W0259802

CHUTZPAH

www.penguin.co.uk

Chutzpah

A Memoir of Faith, Sexuality and Daring to Stay

YEHUDIS FLETCHER

doubleday

TRANSWORLD PUBLISHERS
Penguin Random House, One Embassy Gardens,
8 Viaduct Gardens, London SW11 7BW
www.penguin.co.uk

Transworld is part of the Penguin Random House group of companies whose addresses can be found at global.penguinrandomhouse.com

First published in Great Britain in 2025 by Doubleday
an imprint of Transworld Publishers

A CIP catalogue record for this book
is available from the British Library.

ISBN 9780857529954

Typeset in 12/15.5 pt Minion Pro Typeset by Jouve (UK), Milton Keynes
Printed and bound in Great Britain by Clays Ltd, Elcograf S.p.A.

The authorized representative in the EEA is Penguin Random House Ireland, Morrison Chambers, 32 Nassau Street, Dublin D02 YH68.

1

This book is dedicated to all those forced to stay silent

Author's note

The names and other identifying features of the people in this book have been changed, because who am I to tell another's story? I can only tell my own.

A note on terminology

I have used the term Charedi (pronounced kha-ray-dee) to describe the Jewish denomination in which I was brought up. The term Charedi is derived from the Hebrew verb *lechared*, meaning 'to tremble'; the 'ch' sound is soft, as in Bach and *chutzpah*. Charedi literally means 'one who trembles' (before G-d). I still choose to use that term as an identifier, even though some would argue that Charedi describes a set of practices that exclude, for example, being out as a lesbian or women wearing trousers. My decision to identify as part of the Charedi community is simple: I never left, and you can't throw someone out of their own heritage.

The term Charedi is often used interchangeably with 'ultra-orthodox'. I don't like that term because it denotes a hierarchy of religious practice, implying that some Jews are better Jews than others. We aren't.

PROLOGUE

Wash your hands

הַאֱנוֹשׁ מֵאֱלוֹהַ יִצְדָּק אִם מֵעֹשֵׂהוּ יִטְהַר־גָּבֶר

Can mortals be acquitted by G-d? Can man be cleared by his Maker?

Job 4:17

I WAS SIX YEARS OLD and determined to find out if there was actually a G-d.

It was Friday night, the end of the week and the beginning of our weekly sabbath celebrations, and I was facing, head-on, the distinct possibility that He was about to smite me down dead.

The sanctuary at the centre of the synagogue – or *shul*, as we usually called it – that my father, the rabbi, presided over was almost emptied of congregants who had finished their evening prayers and were ready to eat.

Next door, in the *shul* hall, the table was set for dinner, as it was every Friday. The ugly, flat-topped 1960s building stood in stark contrast beside the high stained-glass windows, imposing pillars and arches of the synagogue itself. Each week, my parents headed the two wooden folding tables that had been pushed together to make one wide oblong and my six siblings and I were expected to take our seats alongside a hotchpotch of worshippers who stayed to eat with us after the service. Some were regulars who came again and again, like Samuel, the student with a scraggly ponytail who always had his face buried in a book of psalms, and Felicity, a convert who cried every Friday night on the front step. It was only years later that she worked out that the tears were down to a red wine allergy rather than some kind of religious exaltation. Others were transient, hungry strangers from other Jewish communities looking for a warm meal, like the Australian traveller who, I once clocked with a mix of confusion and appreciation, wore his pyjamas to both the service and dinner that night.

The timing of the sabbath – *shabbos,* to us – is determined by dusk, meaning the exact time it begins varies throughout the year. Invariably, though, it starts twenty minutes before sundown on a Friday evening and ends an hour after sunset on Saturday.

It always felt like a blanket of peace wrapped itself around us when *shabbos* came in. For the next twenty-five hours, the world outside no longer mattered. We weren't to drive, use public transport, write, listen to the radio or use light switches, the telephone, oven or any other form of electricity. Instead, we engaged with family, friends, spirituality and prayer. The change of pace permeated everything and, though it might seem restrictive to others, I loved it.

What I didn't love was the bitterly cold synagogue hall, to

which we decamped for the duration of *shabbos*. My mother preferred to manage it this way, each week setting up sleeping bags on camp beds, and skinny orange-and-brown mattresses, for all nine of my family members because my little sister and I were too small to walk the three miles from home to *shul* and back every Friday night, Saturday morning and Saturday evening for the three services that required my father's and our family's presence.

The hall had cold, polished wood floors that we'd drag each other across, one curled up in the bottom of a sleeping bag, another one or two pulling and spinning on the end then letting go, sending everyone flying. It was a great space to play but terrible to sleep in and I grew to hate how much time I spent there. I hated how cold it was. I hated how bloody freezing the water was that came out of the taps in the ladies' toilets and I hated drying my hands on the rough, green paper towels that turned to sludge between your fingers.

The Friday-night meal would start with a blessing over sacramental wine, then a further blessing over the two golden, braided challah loaves that my mother baked every week and that my father would slice and pass around the table to his guests. But before eating bread, everyone had to wash their hands. Not with soap and not to ensure cleanliness, but to ensure ritual purity. Hand-cleansing was done to a specific rhythm for different occasions, each dictated by religious laws. There were many reasons for washing in our religious lives but, when breaking bread, it was cold water poured twice over the right hand, then twice over the left. This water couldn't come directly from a tap; we had to use a cup to pour it; a cup with a smooth rim and no lip.

The consequences of eating bread with unclean hands were never spelled out to me in detail. It was just one of the thousands of practices that I knew when to carry out and how, one of a myriad rules that I could recite by heart. Questioning these rules felt heretical. But I did question them. I questioned them in my head all the time, even as a small child, and it made me feel like a sinner. It was a sensation I battled with every day, and it was that very feeling of unworthiness that pushed me to put my plan into action. If nothing happened, if lightning didn't strike, maybe I wasn't such a bad little girl, after all. And if it did? Well, I felt that was a risk worth taking.

I resolved to test the extent to which G-d cared about the small actions I took, the little demands that I complied with. Tonight, I wasn't going to wash my hands. I was going to eat bread, impure.

I had one problem, however. I couldn't tell a lie.

Even if everything panned out neatly with G-d, and He did not strike me down dead, my mother might, because, as sure as the water that came out of those toilet taps would be sub-four degrees Celsius, my mother would ask each of us, every mealtime: 'Have you washed?'

Challenging G-d seemed to sit well with me, but fibbing to my mother went against my moral compass. I simply couldn't lie to her. So, I resolved, I would wash my hands. But I would do so at a Fisher Price toy kitchen, its mucky white plastic sink, peeling window scene and phone cradle orphaned of its play receiver would serve as my ruse. I would 'wash' under its make-believe taps: real to me, a child, and just ritualistic enough that I'd be able to nod at my mother: 'Yes, I have washed my hands.'

I was confident that my plan would work because, between washing and eating challah, we weren't allowed to speak – a sign of respect for the bread and in turn for G-d's provision of sustenance. Any delay caused by talking would render the hand-washing invalid. So, I wouldn't have to worry about stammering or blushing while telling my half-lie.

I went through the logistics in my head. The toy kitchen was one floor up from the main hall, in the nursery that doubled as my classroom during the week, at the end of the long corridor that ran from the top of the stairs. I stood, looking up at my mother as she rested in her chair, enjoying those peaceful moments before the congregation returned from prayers. This was my window.

The only thing left to do was to check whether my mother loved me, to make clear to myself what I risked losing before I did something she would find devastating.

'Mummy,' I said, sidling over, my shoes squeaking on the polished floor.

Mummy was quiet, her prayer book resting open in her hands, her eyes almost closed. She looked beautiful. I didn't think I would ever look that beautiful, even when I grew up.

'Mummy,' I repeated, almost a question.

This time she opened her eyes. Angry eyes. Regret rose in my throat. She didn't shout, it was more of a moan, a groan to the G-d who had answered her prayers when she had asked for children but then also kept reminding her of how grateful she should be for them.

My mother had her own routine. The hiatus before she had to host and serve food for family, parishioners and strangers, which she always did with astounding ease, was one of serenity. Each week, in those moments, she would slip off the black mules that she and every other religious Jewish woman her age wore – a wedged heel so slight as to render it absolutely pointless – and sit back on the single easy chair that my father made sure was there for her. She would hold, and sometimes pray from, her small prayer book and warm her stockinged feet on one of the many gas heaters that failed to rid the room of the biting cold. In those moments, I viewed my mother as a queen, serene and enveloped in a pocket of warmth and prayer. I wanted that level of knowing, the security she had in her belief. I had to have it.

'Can't you leave me alone for five minutes?' came her weary, disappointing but not altogether surprising reply. I left her alone and pressed on.

My father was due back from *shul* with his worshippers any minute now and my opportunity was fast approaching. I looked again at Mummy, resplendent, position unchanged, and headed along the downstairs corridor, past the cold ladies' toilets, up the stairs, past the bridal suite at the top, and down the corridor, all the way to the end. I arrived at the wooden classroom door with its window of criss-crossed shatterproof glass that I wasn't quite tall enough to see through. I pushed down on the handle and opened the door into the room, a black vector filled with toys, a place so familiar to me, made awkward by the dark. No one was meant to sleep in the nursery so my father hadn't set a timer for the light switch in this room, but a nightlight in the corridor threw a weak beam through the cloudy glass panel. I tripped over the rubbery edge of the mat that my classmates and I sat on at circle time and recovered myself, noticing my shadow on the wall as I did so. It made me feel less alone. I was acutely aware of the clock on the wall ticking faster and louder than I'd heard it before.

Downstairs, I could hear the group returning from prayers and pictured my mother's rest coming to an end. I knew my father would soon summon us all for *kiddush*, the prayers said over the wine. I needed to be downstairs, in my seat, by then, which meant I had perhaps two minutes to carry out my task. After the wine, when everyone else went to wash their hands, I would mill around, as though I was doing the same, then return to my seat, as they did.

In the classroom, I felt my way forward through the dark, my shoes squeaking again as I slid them over the tiles to avoid tripping. My head hurt inside. I flexed my little fingers in front of me and pushed my glasses up my nose, then scrunched my sleeves up my arms to keep them dry from the play water that was about to rush out of the play taps. I turned them both on, twisting them all the way around and imagining water pouring out hard. I stopped momentarily because there was no cup without a lip but I had no time to waste. I made do without, wiggling each hand under the stream of nothing. My right hand twice, then the same for my left.

As I stepped back, the air around me was still. Inside, I was rushing with the enormity of the sin I was about to commit. I could feel the heat of my blood pumping in every part of my body. I turned and ran out of the nursery, leaving the door wide open, and raced back through the corridor. I couldn't quite hear if the rise of the guests' voices, exuberant from prayer and anticipating dinner, had fallen into silence yet, or if their wood-and-vinyl chairs had been scraped into place at the table. Nor could I quite gauge how much time I had left. I scampered into the hall, slowing my pace as I entered. I could hear my heart beating and wondered if others could too. My mother hadn't noticed I was gone and my father, impatient to start, gestured to me to sit down. No words. I found a seat far away from him.

I was proud of myself for being so clever. In fact, a smile even threatened to spread across my face. My experiment was about to test the fear I had in G-d; to push it to a natural conclusion. In my family, G-d was not only revered, He was the shape of everything we did. G-d wasn't a belief system, He was the rhythm to our home, our lives. I had learned that my happiness was measured only against whether G-d was happy with me. My own experiences and emotions were irrelevant. G-d was the ultimate parent whose approval I needed. But, given that G-d was theoretical, when I spoke with Him on my own, in my mind, I could imagine His responses, and His approval if I needed to as well. With my Fisher Price dare, I'd found a grey area in which I was able to imagine that He approved.

My parents were my main concern now. If they caught me, or my siblings caught me and told them, I would have to confess my half-lie and that made me afraid.

As I sat down at the table, I was certain I'd be called out at any moment. Was I a little bit late? Had I taken a little bit too long? I imagined my father seeing through my ruse and exposing me in front of everyone for a sin I hadn't even managed to finish. Would he banish me from his table, hungry and cold? Or worse, would he dismiss my sin completely, as if I was too little and inconsequential for it to matter?

I imagined the all-seeing, all-knowing G-d exposing me, opening the ground beneath my seat, swallowing me, destroying me. I was uncomfortably aware of my own conspicuousness. I felt my bottom shift in the chair, its black vinyl covering making the slight farting sound it produced whenever someone took their seat. I was sure my father had clocked something was off when he'd gestured to me to sit. I don't know what he thought I'd been doing but his glance made me nervous. It would have been so easy to cave, to get up and run away embarrassed, childish, but I wanted to stay. I wanted to believe.

Armed with my half-truth, half-lie, I listened to him bless the wine, thanking G-d, and then shepherding everyone out to wash their hands under the glacial water – in the men's toilets and the ladies' toilets, in the huge sinks in the industrial kitchen or the small aluminium sink in the caretaker's cupboard. Everyone scattered in different directions. No one paid much attention to me at the best of times; that evening, for once, I was grateful for my invisibility. I kept watch and returned to the table alongside everyone else, taking my seat, ready to finish my sin.

Each moment that passed was an eternity. My father took his place last. Silence. He uncovered the two braided loaves, golden with egg wash, and lifted them together. He said the blessing with his eyes closed to prevent him from seeing anything immodest while at prayer: 'Blessed are you, G-d, Lord Almighty, who brings forth bread from the earth.'

He started to slice – the right loaf before the left, because the Talmud, the cannon of rabbinical teachings that tell us how to live by Judaism's central text, the Torah, tells us to – doing so in his idiosyncratic way that even then I found quite maddening. Still, no one spoke. My mother loved that time – the only time she wasn't disturbed. I think my father prolonged it for her. The hush filled my ears in whatever space my roaring heartbeat left for it. The basket of bread was passed around the table, first to my mother, then to the guests, then to the children, in age order.

I was the second youngest at the table alongside my five older siblings: Miriam and Dov Ber, who were twins, a girl and a boy aged fifteen; my sister Leah and brother Shmuel, who were seven and six years older than me; our brother Elchanan, who was nine at the time; then there was me, six, and my little sister Devorah, three.

I held my slice, aware that I was supposed to be eating it as soon as possible, to prevent delay and disrespect, my cheeks and my left ear betraying me by flushing red. I didn't know who could tell or who was looking because I was desperate not to make eye contact. The consequences of challenging my parents, let alone G-d, were unknown and the distinct possibility that I was about to face some terrible, biblical punishment remained as real to me as the drawings I coloured in of men in the Old Testament stories being swallowed by the ground or consumed by fire for irreligious doings.

My moment of truth was here. Poppy seeds tumbled from the bread's crust as I raised it to my mouth. I scraped them with my teeth but I didn't bite, not yet. Until my first bite, my sin remained incomplete. The seeds felt rough on my tongue. My mother's challah was never sweet. Her mother was diabetic so she always left out the sugar, which is what makes most people, Jewish or otherwise, love its taste. I brought my teeth together on either side of my slice, bit down and forced a small piece of its doughy interior into my mouth, past the lump in my throat. My knees locked and I jolted myself upright to swallow. Nothing happened.

I took another bite. Nothing. And another. Still nothing.

I could hear my father talking to our guests about the Torah portion of the week, delivering his teaching on the meaning of the Bible passage he would read in synagogue the next day. Then, I saw my mother distributing slices of gefilte fish, a dish of poached ground haddock and whiting, with dollops of our family favourite, avocado mashed with boiled eggs and garlic. She had set a green salad on the table along with bowls of mayonnaise and *chrein* – horseradish and beetroot sauce – which my brothers were fighting over. It was like every other Friday night. No one knew.

I had eaten bread with unclean hands and not a single thing had changed. I was invincible now. Layers of restriction fell away, replaced by what felt, to six-year-old me, like endless possibility and opportunity. I had barely started school but I had already discovered it was possible to rebel – from right there, where I sat.

1

Jolly good fellow, Part 1

אִוֶּלֶת קְשׁוּרָה בְלֶב־נָעַר שֵׁבֶט מוּסָר יַרְחִיקֶנָּה מִמֶּנּוּ

If folly settles in the heart of a child, the rod of discipline will remove it.

Proverbs 22:15

I BEGAN MY GENESIS BY almost killing my mother. Or, at least, that is what she told me many times; how, on 28 August 1987, at the Rutherglen Maternity Hospital in Stonelaw Road, South Lanarkshire, she could have died having me.

I was a fat, ruddy baby taken to a three-bedroom sandstone terrace with a kitchen extension that was falling off the back. I shared my home with my parents, five older siblings, and a constant flow of my father's parishioners.

Babies are, of course, born perfect and free from sin. But my family subscribed to the Charedi teaching that as soon as any person, even a newborn, sleeps, one sixtieth of their soul leaves their body and, when they wake, the impurity of death rests between their fingers. This means that I would not have been a day old before my father rolled up his white shirt cuffs, tucked me under his arm and washed my little balled-up fists, translucent with the newness of birth, for the first time, over the small porcelain sink in the hospital ward.

They gave me the name Yehudis, the Hebrew for 'Judith', followed by the middle name Gittel, meaning 'good' in Yiddish. We didn't speak the old European dialect but my mother, like other Charedi Jews, was nostalgic towards it. My brothers called me Little Gittel. When my mother was approving, she called me Judy Trudy. When she didn't like my behaviour, I was Dirty Girty. Often, she was talking about me, not to me.

As a little girl, I was the perfect picture of Charedi Jewish childhood. I wore polyester dresses with opaque tights bobbly from too many washes, with not an inch of flesh beyond my elbows or collarbone exposed to the sinful male gaze. I had awkward, big middle teeth, a sturdy little body and pale-blue plastic glasses with tiny white stripes that I'd worn since I was three. My hair fell in coarse Semitic curls, auburn-brown with a heavy, unruly fringe that my mother cut herself as I stood in the bathtub with a piece of Sellotape above my eyebrows as a spirit level.

But as far as my personality went, I was an old soul who experienced responsibility directly and urgently because my worthiness and usefulness within my large family depended on it. The seven siblings of the Fletcher household were split into two groups: the older five, born within five years of one another, and the younger two, me and Devorah. This made me the eldest of the little ones; a de facto leader expected to let Devorah have whatever she wanted, never to fight and to always give in. I was never granted the privileges that came with being the baby of the family. Our family called me the 'pocket-sized professor' and Devorah the 'bite-sized' one. They laughed at Devorah's jokes but mine were discarded as precocious and annoying. When she cried, my mother tended to her. When I cried, she told me: 'Turn the taps off!'

My family didn't really know what to do with me. I wasn't quite disrespectful or outspoken enough to be punished but I didn't conform to the demure behaviour expected of a Charedi Jewish girl, either. Because of this, most of them wavered between ignoring me and cutting me down to size.

Sometimes, I got tired of being quiet. One Friday-night dinner, when I was seven, as guests tucked into their boiled chicken, I listened in to the adults discussing women's representation in Judaism. Our guests suggested that women were denigrated and my mother spluttered a defence. I inserted myself into their conversation.

'Mr Howard,' I piped up. 'When you say that, you are the one ignoring the achievements of women like Bruriah and Deborah.' Bruriah was a female sage who learned Torah with the men in ancient times; Deborah was a prophetess. I emulated them both but should have known, from my father's glare, that involving myself in the adults' conversation would be met with his disapproval.

Growing up, my world consisted of my home, *shul* and school, and those last two were in the same building. On the odd Thursday night, Mummy might pack boiled eggs and fried fish balls and we'd eat supper in the local park for a treat, and there was the occasional suitable outing to a stately home. Other than that, my world remained rather small.

The house was my mother's domain. Like other religious women, she wore a *sheitel* – a wig to preserve her modesty, keeping her real hair meticulously covered from the view of any man but her husband. Hers was short, brunette and cut in a pageboy style. But neither of my parents had been raised in a house as religious as the one they now ran. They were brought up in kosher, Jewish homes where observance was cultural rather than prescribed: *shabbos* dinners on Friday nights but football matches on Saturday afternoons. Daddy hadn't been to university but Mummy had and qualified as an English teacher. Neither found their heightened level of orthodoxy until their early twenties, after taking gap years in Israel. They chose to raise their own family within a small, quaint community that followed the most extreme interpretation of Jewish law and sought to protect us from secular influences. Those influences included the more liberal Jewish families who lived near us, even the ones my father ministered to, who knew a freer and less austere life than we did.

Our house had an eternally yeasty smell that emanated from my mother's frequent bread-baking, including her sugarless Friday-night challah loaves. When it was peaceful the hum of Radio 4, one of the few secular entertainments she permitted herself, could be heard from the kitchen. If she was happy, she'd sing the theme tune to *The Archers*, making up a stream of nonsense lyrics while kneading dough for the bread she made for our lunchtime sandwiches. Being of short stature, she'd stand on a small, plastic stool to give herself the benefit of height and mix one part stoneground, wholemeal flour with one part bleached, white flour, to get the perfect blend of goodness and fluff, pummelling it into a smooth, springy ball. Once they were baked, she would store the loaves in one of the large brown-paper bags that hung on a nail in our kitchen wall, bought from a wholesaler who prayed at the synagogue.

My mother cooked other food but bread was our staple and I loved it, especially served warm from the oven. Nine of us were surviving on a rabbi's salary and were what you might describe as 'middle-class poor': we had stability, owned our home and car, but everything was threadbare and food portions were carefully calculated. It must have been exhausting for my mother to spread everything so thinly, and her tiredness showed. Her brow was permanently furrowed. We usually ate one hot meal a day; the rest was either Weetabix or bread that twice weekly was accompanied by protein: a rollmop herring or thin slice of Cheddar cheese per child. This fairly mundane diet meant that I lived for the cheese. On the other days we had Marmite, peanut butter (salt- and sugar-free), jam, sunflower-seed butter or margarine and her perpetual, under-salted vegetable soup, cooked on Monday and reheated until Thursday. Eating that felt like giving in, so I never did.

Bananas were available daily and encouraged, but always halved, so we had to find someone to split one with. Mummy often ate Ryvita crackers and used her banana stump to mop up the crumbs. If I heard her ask, 'Would anyone like to share a banana with me?' I would jump at the chance for a tender moment, shared.

We never ate out – nowhere in Glasgow was kosher enough anyway. Only on *shabbos*, when we hosted our synagogue guests, would there be a little more indulgence. My mother would spend Fridays boiling chickens and filling huge Thermoses with warm, homemade chicken soup glistening with fat bubbles, which she'd then stack into the footwells of my father's copper-brown Space Cruiser to transport to the synagogue. The boiled soup would sweat and spill its juices under the feet of us seven children as we whirled down the road.

I shared a bedroom with my older sisters, Miriam and Leah. Leah was seven years my senior and too busy to even look my way. She spent most of her time doing whatever she could to curry our mother's favour. Miriam, on the other hand, the eldest child and the girl half of the twins, argued with Mummy. There were nine years separating Miriam and me, and we both had dark hair and big mouths. Despite the age gap, she was my ally, and I hers. But beyond the two of us, I felt unloved within our family from a very young age. While my mother told me she loved me, it rarely translated into actions. I was always looking for it – love – betraying myself to earn it in the form of approval if not actual affection.

There were religious expectations on all of us, different rules for girls and boys that fed into an intricately layered system of how we were expected to conduct ourselves during every waking moment. Miriam was as devout as she was expected to be but we both shared a deep sense of justice and a mutual understanding of the world as an adventure. I relied on her to mother me and validate me in ways that others didn't and I adored her for how she made me feel.

It was my father who looked after my practical needs most. When I was very young, it was he – a slim, tall man with a full, short, dark-brown beard and rabbi's uniform of everyday black suit, thin dark tie and white shirt – who would bathe me, brush my hair and teeth, and get me ready for bed. He never really talked to me through all this but he sang funny songs about observing the commandments or preparing for holy days, set to tunes like 'Jingle Bells' or football chants that we had obviously never heard. 'Glory, glory, clean the dishes/Everybody obeys Mummy's wishes.'

On Tuesdays, Daddy taught a Torah class for local men, held in our dining room. I would knock on the door and be permitted to enter. In my pale-blue, long-sleeved, modest nightie, I would say goodnight and kiss him, although he never kissed me back. He kissed me only once a week, on the top of my head, after saying the children's blessing over me on a Friday night. 'May you be like Sarah, Rebecca, Rachel and Leah,' he'd whisper, holding his hands in a canopy over each of his daughters in turn, asking G-d to secure our futures as wives and mothers, just like our biblical foremothers.

Sometimes, if my mother was busy, I accompanied him to the synagogue, where we'd enter through the enormous arched doorway to the foyer fortified by Roman-style pillars. The synagogue was an imposing and, naturally, holy sight. With its Romanesque pink brick, domed atrium and high double doorway it commanded attention and reverence. It had originally been modelled on a great baroque *shul* in Amsterdam and was built at the turn of the twentieth century when Anglo-Jewry decided they needed such grand places of worship. Inside, it could seat hundreds of people but most services saw only twenty or so from our provincial community.

When there was no one around, my father would let me

inside the prayer hall, the sanctuary where he led services from the raised platform, the *bimah*, in the centre. As a girl, I wasn't really allowed to be in there, especially not during prayer time. This was a men's space, grand with navy-blue velvet seats and gilt trim. Women prayed and watched from seats on the balcony above, separated for fear they would tempt the men away from their prayer. During services, I would sit next to my mother, looking down at the men, in two minds as to whether I was lucky not to perform, to sing and be on display, or annoyed at being left out of important proceedings. My mother wasn't confused at all – she sat where she could catch my father's eye when he read a verse they both found meaningful or funny.

My father's occasional tacit permission to enter wasn't enough to satisfy my appetite for inclusion. Every opportunity I had – if he took a call in the office or had to tend to some other business – I'd steal into the prayer hall and pour my heart out. I'd stand in front of the ornate marble ark, the forty-foot holy enclave at the end of the *shul* that held the Torah scrolls, and press my hands against its velvet curtain, which only men were meant to touch – it was majestic, like a fixture in a fairy-tale castle. If Daddy caught me, he presumed I was playing. But I was praying. I was desperate – for answers to the many questions I had about my life that looked so solid and rule-filled to others but felt so precarious to me; for explanations that might soothe the frustrations I felt at home; for love. That place was the centre of power as I saw it and I wanted to stay there. If only I could have more time, perhaps my side of the story could be heard.

'G-d always listens, Yehudis Gittel,' my mother would tell

me, observing my ambition to grasp more. 'Sometimes the answer is "no". You have to be willing to hear that.'

When my prayers weren't heard, I cried. I cried over the injustices a little girl feels – when Devorah got a bigger piece of cheese or when my mother said something belittling to me. I also cried because no one answered my questions about the Bible. How was it OK for the matriarch, Rebecca, to have been married at the age of three? How could she lift heavy water jugs and feed all those camels on her own? No one took my questions seriously. In fact, I often heard my parents preaching that religious questions only existed on a physical level. In the spiritual world, there were no questions, but for people not quite on that level, there were answers for everything. All I had to do was acknowledge that the ones they provided were the right ones.

On the rare occasion that they entertained my doubts, I wasn't satisfied by their answers.

'I'm hurting,' I would tell my mother.

'I'm praying for you,' she'd reply.

'But G-d isn't answering your prayers, Mummy. I'm still hurting.' I'd cry some more.

I asked G-d for lots of things in that space. He always said 'no'.

Shul was an extension of home. I spent 9 a.m. to 4 p.m. being schooled there every day in the ice-cold classrooms that smelled of cleaning products and wax crayons, above the hall. There were barely twenty students – just me and my siblings and a handful of other children from the area who, like us, were too religious for the local authority schools. Even the sole Jewish school in the area was deemed too lax for our family's standards. Our group's numbers were inflated by a crèche made up of our teachers' babies and toddlers. The staff at our little school were part of the furniture of my life: Mrs Boyle the cleaner, quiet and ever-present with a mop and bucket but whom we knew nothing about; Mrs Fox, from Dublin, who ran the *shul* office and would occasionally produce a Quality Street from her pocket, where she stashed them like brightly coloured jewels; her husband, Mr Fox, the synagogue chairman; and our headteacher, Mrs Silver, a tall, thin woman with a synthetic, wiry black wig and the softest skin. Mrs Silver wore thick beige tights under sandals no matter the weather, and taught us girls to read and chant Torah verses just like the boys did, which was very rare within a Charedi environment. In hindsight, she was one of the first Charedi feminists I knew.

We didn't take the bus to school. Mummy taught English to the girls and my father taught the older boys Talmud, so we'd travel there together in the Space Cruiser, while other students were picked up in the clapped-out blue sixteen-seater minibus which my mother deemed too unsafe for her own children. It was driven by Mrs Levy, who worked in the nursery, and each child along the route would clamber in, finding a seat or a place on the wooden planks balanced across the gangway to provide as much seating as possible. The minibus would head through inner-city Glasgow, past the old tenement buildings and the BT exchange. The teachers, who also took the minibus, each had a seat and piled babies on their laps, brushed children's hair and spooned breakfast into little mouths while the bus bounced through morning traffic and chugged up the steep hill to *shul*.

I longed to travel on the bus with my friends. Instead, I'd

meet them in the classroom-cum-nursery with the Fisher Price kitchen. The walls were decorated with our artwork and posters teaching us what prayers to say and when: blessings before we ate various foods or the thanks to give after we went to the toilet; the blessing to give during thunder and lightning, and the sharp rebuke to be recited if we saw a rainbow, a reminder from G-d to never again descend to the depths of depravity that caused His biblical flood. A colourful wooden slide was built against one wall, against another there was a play corner and coat hooks, and, in the centre, the circle-time mat that I'd tripped over on my way to challenge G-d.

At lunchtime I'd unfurl a packed lunch – sandwiches of four slices of Mummy's homemade bread with Marmite or peanut butter. On cheese day, I'd open them out and toast them on the gas heater, the same one she used to warm her feet. On Fridays in deep winter when nightfall was as early as 3.30 p.m., we would finish school early to prepare for *shabbos*, each receiving a boiled sweet from our teacher in recognition of this special day. I'd hold it in my hand the whole way home, rustling its wrapper with my fingertips, digging its sharp plastic twists into my palm. Once home, I'd make eye contact with my mother then do as her eyes asked and drop it into the freshly emptied bin, gaining a prune and her approval in return.

'Sugar rots your teeth,' she would tell us. 'Good parents don't let their children ruin the body G-d gave them.' I obliged because I wanted my mother's approval more than I wanted the sweet, and together we enjoyed the superiority we felt over other families, who didn't eat as sensibly as we did.

Class sizes at school were a moveable feast that met the

community's needs. The nursery catered for babies and toddlers, including Devorah, while 'little ones' learned together in a class of five that was made up of me, two other girls and two boys. My older sisters and brothers were scattered among classes with children approximately the same age as them who were split into boys and girls from the age of about six, when boys were deemed ready to examine religious texts, which girls weren't allowed to look at – the Talmud instructs: 'Whoever teaches their daughters Talmud, it is as if they have taught them prostitution.'

The other girls in the school wore cheap, plastic Mary-Jane shoes but I had red leather ones with white stitching and thick cream laces. My community said only boys wore lace-up shoes but I had a mother who wanted my feet to be healthy and my bones strong.

'Run to do good deeds in them,' she said when she bought them for me from Alan Mickel, the shoe shop in the smarter part of town.

A boy named Yoel was my main friend. He had golden hair, a soft face and grubby nails, a combination I found unthreatening. He was my school 'husband' and we'd spend break times racing one another across the playground, which was concrete and pebbly, and devoid of anything as frivolous as toys or play equipment. Just inside the synagogue fence, to the left of the entrance, was an enormous old tree with knotted roots that splayed outwards, weaving overground. The way they entangled with one another created a space, towards the middle, to sit – a magical and precious private place carpeted with helicopter seeds that became my safety spot, a bolthole for when I needed somewhere to call my own, something I distinctly lacked elsewhere. I'd sit in my tree and send Yoel to find me wildflowers, which we pretended were cabbages. He did everything I asked but rarely well enough for my exacting standards.

I didn't have any other good friends. I was more interested in adult conversation than childish prattle, but the adults weren't interested in me. I was growing into a geeky kid. By the age of seven, I was already sharply aware of what everyone else was doing and saying. And I was commenting on it – so much so that I appeared to constantly irritate everyone around me, particularly my parents.

In lessons, we learned the Hebrew alphabet, the week's Torah story or the 613 commandments of Jewish law by rote from little plastic cards. The teacher would time us reading Hebrew. Whoever finished their page of letters within sixty seconds could choose a sticker from her sheet. The stickers were more Hebrew letters, and Yoel and I were in competition for the only 'yud', the Y-equivalent that started both of our names. Luckily for me, he wasn't much competition. The rest of the time I was expected to play with dolls or the toy kitchen and not to think or care too deeply about what I was being taught. While the boys were meant to be studious, we girls were expected to be easy-going, but my thirst for knowledge and my mother's passion for English meant that I read English long before the others did, and better than my Hebrew. My mother encouraged me to read the books we were given on Jewish festivals and didn't disapprove when I wrote down stories that I dreamed up in my imagination: 'Publish, Doodis, publish,' she would say, calling me by the baby name that had stuck since my first attempts to pronounce Yehudis. Eventually, I began to develop a liking for correcting others' speech.

'I can give you a answer,' an older girl would say.

'*An* answer,' I would offer primly.

I was dismissed as clever by teachers, family and classmates, and it wasn't said kindly; I thought too deeply about things and that was deemed awkward. I annoyed people.

When I was five and my classmates were still learning their ABC, my teacher gave me copies of *The Secret Garden* and *The Railway Children*, which I read over and over at the back of the classroom. I read constantly, and anything – a shampoo bottle while sitting on the toilet, the back of a bag of flour, even the books my mother used to teach brides about being a good wife.

Inside our home, only religious or religious-adjacent texts were allowed, so it was stuffed full of old Jewish novels, biographies of holy people and tales of miraculous rabbis who had healed sick widows. The exceptions to this were the *Tintin* and *Asterix* books that my brothers were allowed to borrow from the library. There's absolutely no reason why these were permissible over anything else but there were anomalies everywhere in my life. What they weren't allowed were *Hardy Boys* books, because they were 'violent', but they acquired them anyhow and hid them behind the ladder to the loft, so I'd whistle through those, too. I didn't understand how the boys got to be 'The Boys'. They had allowances that my sisters and I did not. They could show chutzpah to my parents, arriving late for supper or answering back, and get away with it, while I watched Miriam get in trouble for behaving the exact same way. And of course, as girls, we had more stringent modesty rules, which required us to cover our bodies from our elbows to our collarbones and toes, even as children.

In the mornings, I wasn't welcome at the breakfast table until I'd said my prayers. Each day, I'd stride purposefully downstairs and make sure that someone saw me pick up my prayer book and take it back up with me. In the privacy of my room, I'd set it down carefully on a pillow and sit on my bed because we weren't allowed to sit on the same surface as a holy book out of respect for G-d's name. For twenty-five minutes, which I calculated to be the appropriate, unsuspicious amount of time to 'pray', I'd ignore my prayer book and read something else. I lived in fear that someone would check on me, or worse still that they'd ask if I'd prayed, because I wouldn't have been able to deny that I hadn't. As I returned downstairs, I would mutter fervently under my breath: 'Please G-d, please G-d, don't let anyone catch me.' But it wasn't G-d's anger that I was scared of; it was my mother's.

There were very few frills in our house. Apart from the birth of my younger sister, which we celebrated in the hospital ward with kosher choc ices and lemonade, birthdays in my family were far from indulgent. After all, the only birthday mentioned in the Torah was Pharoah's and he wasn't even Jewish. They were usually marked with a '*Mazel tov*' and cards from my two grandmas, both in Manchester – Grandma J on my father's side and Grandma G on my mother's side – and from my great-grandma Dolly, who always sent a fiver. Cake was not normally a thing; that would have involved too much effort from my mother. So, when I came home from school on my eighth birthday to find Miriam hunched over the counter in our tiny avocado-tiled kitchen, unfurling greaseproof paper from a dark chocolate figure-of-eight she'd made just for me, I couldn't believe it.

It was the last Monday of August 1995. By now we had moved to a different house, a six-minute drive away and closer to the three other families who were as religious as ours. Here, I shared most of the girls' room with my sisters, the remainder sectioned off by plasterboard creating a demi-room big enough for a single bed where guests stayed. Ours was a kosher house, where any religious person passing through Glasgow was welcome. Rabbis, Grandma G and a jewellery salesman, introduced to us as Uncle Shimon, each often stayed on the other side of that drywall.

Miriam was setting out my eighth-birthday creation on our mother's white-and-brown, oval melamine plate – not a weekday plate but not the best china, either. She carried it from the kitchen, through the living room – which we for some reason called the home room – with its heaving orange couches and piles of clutter, and into the dining room. I walked behind her, my eyes fixed on the belt at the back of her dress. Miriam looked over to me as she set the plate down on the dining room table. Never before had my birthday been celebrated in the dining room. Its heavy wooden table demanded decorum and conformity. It was where my father had written a thousand sermons and where guests gathered to eat or learn from the rabbi and his wife. I didn't know who owned that table to begin with but I knew my parents had salvaged it from a skip and elevated it to something holy. Miriam extended it to its full length.

'Why have you done this?' I asked.

'Because I want to – for you.'

I held Miriam's hand – hers strong and soft, mine the same but in miniature – then bolted upstairs to change into my green *shabbos* dress – high neck, sleeves below the elbow, too thick for summer but suitable for a celebration. I placed a floral headband in my curly brown hair, which had now grown to chin length, and looked in the mirror inside the tallboy where we stored our clothes. I felt good. I closed my eyes and pictured my 'eight', counting off the colourful kosher Smarties that studded its glossy top. The extravagance. I felt like a queen.

Downstairs, my father sat at the head of the table as always and my mother at the foot, the rest of us around it. Everyone knew their place, literally and figuratively. Usually, my mother told me to sit near the door so I could get up easily to help serve and clear. That day, I was bestowed the honour of sitting next to my father.

A copy of the Talmud – more or less the entirety of Jewish law and legend – stared down at me from the main bookshelf. The table was laid with a white cloth. When I look back at photos, the joy from my electric, gap-toothed smile rises from the printed picture.

I wasn't at all used to sitting beside my father. I was a child who chafed against the edges of what was expected of me, who always needed and wanted more love than was being offered, and it was because of this that my father kept me at a distance. You'd think by now that I'd have been used to not meeting my father's expectations but that afternoon, as the sun slowly softened the chocolate and my family sang 'Happy Birthday', my father's disapproval broke my heart. I don't remember doing anything wrong or naughty but, as they reached their encore of 'For she's a jolly good fellow', my father tweaked the words.

'For she's *going* to be a jolly good fellow,' he sang, his mouth wide with false cheer.

'She's *going* to be a jolly good fellow,' I heard him sing again. And again.

I stopped singing, my swinging legs coming abruptly to a halt under the table. Wasn't I a jolly good fellow already? Wasn't it an unwritten, universally accepted rule that every person was celebrated on their birthday for exactly who they were?

My joy evaporated. My heart hurt. I must have misheard him. Maybe he was objecting to my loudness? Or my exuberant self-promotion? Maybe it wasn't intended as a rebuke after all. I looked around the table to try to understand. My mother and brothers fell into step with his lyrics.

'For she's *going* to be a jolly good fellow,' they were singing, though more solemnly than my father.

Devorah sucked her two middle fingers quietly. Leah and Miriam remained silent; girls over twelve are not permitted to raise their voices in song, even in front of their own father, because, as the teachings say, *kol b'isha erva*: 'A woman's voice is her nakedness.' I knew that, but I pretended their silence was in solidarity with the stinging pain I now felt. No one looked at me. Maybe they thought it would make me feel less ashamed. Maybe they agreed with him. A film of tears formed behind my glasses. All I could see – then and now – is that no one stood up for me.

The words rushed through my ears. Maybe he smiled to

convince my siblings and mother that this was OK, to normalize hurting his little girl's feelings, squashing her spirit, embarrassing her. Tears ran down the back of my throat. My green dress felt tight and hot, and my skin prickled under the acrylic.

I felt obliged to take his rebuke and thank him for it. I still feel that obligation. So, I smiled, wider and wider. I would be damned if anyone was going to make me cry on my birthday. I focused on the 'eight'. Miriam knew I was a jolly good fellow. From the rest of them, the love I received that day, and on many more to come, was always wrapped up in rejection.

2

The wonder of becoming you

לֹא בַשָּׁמַיִם הִוא . . . כִּי־קָרוֹב אֵלֶיךָ הַדָּבָר מְאֹד

It's not in the heavens . . . No, the thing is very close to you.

Deuteronomy 30:12–13

I'd been up for over an hour when my mother came down, around 7 a.m., to find me inspecting books at the dining room table. I was nine years old. It was wintertime and still dark outside but I'd woken earlier than everyone else.

Mummy leaned against the low wooden sideboard containing the second-best Royal Doulton china that we used for meat meals every *shabbos* and the third-best Royal Doulton that we used for milky, unheated meals every Saturday afternoon, when we hosted the *shabbos* afternoon meal – depending on the time of year, either a high tea or a bigger supper – at home. Jewish law doesn't permit meat and milk to mix. (Incidentally, there was a very-best china set, a wedding present of my parents' that had sat unused for two decades until my sister Miriam's recent engagement, the first occasion in our lives deemed enough of an event to eat from it.)

Mummy was facing the other way when she asked me: 'Yehudis Gittel, do you know how many holes you have in your bottom?'

Now I knew why she had her back to me.

'Two,' I said.

'No,' she corrected. 'It's three.' Her tone was clipped and functional, as if she was irritated that it was her duty to have this conversation. Finding me alone presented an opportunity to get it over and done with.

'The third one is called a vagina and it's between the two you already know about,' she continued, speaking into the other side of the room. 'The reason you have it is to help you have children one day.'

This was interesting.

She explained that I would bleed monthly to prepare for this and turned to hand me a slim book with a purple cover featuring a drawing of a modestly dressed blonde girl blowing a dandelion: *The Wonder of Becoming You: How a Jewish Girl Grows Up*, by Dr Miriam Grossman. I studied it.

'Will you learn this with me?' I asked. I had a vision of her sitting next to me, teaching me the way she taught her brides.

Mummy met my eyes briefly and agreed – but she never did follow up on her promise. I, however, excited at the prospect of brand-new information, read it from cover to cover that evening after school. And the next night. And the next. The book explained how my uterus was shaped like a pear, that I should do jumping jacks when I was on my period to relieve pain, and that starting my period was confirmation that I would be able to have babies. Unsurprisingly, it left me with more questions than I'd started with and I began searching everywhere for answers. We kept a copy of the *Encyclopaedia Britannica* behind the steps to the attic, where the contraband *Hardy Boys* were hidden, and its hefty volumes were one of the only sources of secular information in the house. I searched for anything I could find about periods and babies. When I visited Grandma J's house, in Manchester, I pored over stacks of *Reader's Digest* that she kept on a wicker bookshelf in her sunroom until I found an article that mentioned 'sex'. Naturally, I had no idea what this word meant but the context of the piece suggested it was relevant, so, when we got home, I looked it up in my mother's *Oxford English Dictionary*. I was flabbergasted by what I discovered and couldn't keep the information to myself.

The next *shabbos*, I called an urgent meeting of the Private Conversation Club, a secret society that I'd established with three girls from school. Spending time in other girls' homes was one of the few accepted social activities I was permitted to participate in. These particular gatherings took place in my friend Mindy's attic. We hadn't even reached the top rung of the steel ladder when the words spilled out.

'Sex is a man putting his penis in a woman's vagina,' I blurted as we frantically pulled up the door to discuss my bombshell further before my curfew. Mindy was eleven and her sister Feigy was thirteen. Tehila, the third girl, was a year younger than me. They were amazed.

For us, sex was the biggest secret. Boys were exposed to mentions in the Talmud but only in an abstract sense. Neither boys nor girls were meant to know anything about it until we were engaged. Then we would be given a class in the days before the wedding, the kind of lesson my mother delivered as part of her role as a rabbi's wife, to prepare us for our wedding night. That was all the sex education we would ever have. Until then, the absence of information only added to the heightened sense that something hot and exciting existed. This is of course how it is for most children but we were expected to go to much greater lengths not to breach the taboo. For us, the silence was supposed to last until we were already engaged to be married, at which point we might still not have been told that consummation was a necessary part of the agreement.

Feigy's mouth was still hanging open when Mindy spoke: 'I can imagine Sheindy doing that with her husband,' she said, referring to their older sister, 'but not Beila.' Beila, another sister, who was exceptionally modest, had five children. So, we deduced with shock, she must've had sex at least five times.

The following Monday, when I got back from school, my mother was waiting.

'What have you done, Yehudis Gittel?' she asked, exasperated. 'I understand why you went off to find that information, but couldn't you keep it to yourself?' She didn't specify which information.

My left ear began to burn. Word had got back to Mummy and she was embarrassed by me.

On Tuesday morning, a woman called Mrs Abramowitz was waiting to have a sex talk with my class – an unprecedented and begrudging attempt at damage control necessitated by me opening my big mouth. Mrs Abramowitz wasn't one of our usual teachers. She wore perfume and high heels, and her wig was blow-dried into a fat, glamorous bob.

By this time, our school had relocated to the top floor of a different *shul* – not an unusual occurrence given the informality of our educational set-up – but the classes and staff were exactly the same. We enjoyed a little secular education when time allowed – some geography and English, French, a little science as long as no one mentioned anything that contradicted creationism. At this point, we were separated from the boys because we were too close to puberty – which counts as adulthood in Jewish law – to mix.

Mrs Abramowitz was a local lady whose home I'd sometimes visited for Friday-night meals; on the rare occasion that my parents were not hosting in the synagogue hall, the invitation would be reciprocated by friends and community members. I'd clocked her wearing black, satin kitten heels with fluffy pompoms, so I felt sure she knew all about sex. Now that she was in my classroom, I was thrilled that my questions would finally be answered. The other girls also seemed to get a kick out of the fact we'd had the power to change the course of events and with such a juicy topic. But rather than expand on what I'd discovered, she taught us only this: that sex was holy and made a marriage special. I was bitterly disappointed – though I was also a little impressed at my ability to send the adults into such a state of panic.

Over the next few years, as I headed towards adolescence, life around me began to change. At home, both of my elder sisters married and moved out, first Miriam and then Leah. Miriam leaving when I wasn't yet a teenager left me especially unsure and insecure. Her husband was seven years older than she was, with a long black beard to his waist, and I saw him only as a person who came between me and her.

He was her priority now and I no longer had her to ground me. Whenever we were together, I'd come up with banal questions for her to ask him on my behalf in an effort to ingratiate myself into their relationship and as an excuse to talk to her. By the time Leah left, a year later, I knew better what I was dealing with, which made the changing family dynamics just a little easier for me to grasp. Miriam was already pregnant by this point and the promise of babies as a result of my sisters marrying at least offered some excitement, given that there would be some cute kids for me to look after and play with.

I was an auntie to a nephew by the time I was ten. This delivered me a little bit of status, as close as I could get to being a mother for now, and sometimes when my parents went away, usually to Israel, they'd leave Devorah and me with Miriam, her husband and the baby in Stamford Hill, at the heart of London's Charedi community, for a couple of weeks at a time. The community there practised an even more stringent version of Judaism than we did. Miriam and her husband conversed in Yiddish and I picked it up. I would change my nephew's nappy and take him for walks in his buggy, past the huge Edwardian terrace houses and the kerbsides bumper-to-bumper with seven-seater cars that belonged to the large religious families who lived there. Miriam cooked me hot, piped mash potato with a crispy top and served afters with every meal, even on weekdays. It was the first time I hadn't been rationed. I think it was her first time, too.

During one stay, I discovered a copy of *What to Expect When You're Expecting* and continued my self-education, but I found it clinical and limited. Dissatisfied, I remained curious – something a good Jewish girl was expected to fight. I embraced it.

By the age of twelve for girls and thirteen for boys, a life of complete separation for the sexes, bar marriage, began. Men existed in another world to women, it seemed. Siblings could be in the same room but beyond that the two sexes socialized, celebrated, learned and even swam separately. Men worked to earn a living and studied Torah while the women in our community weren't even permitted to drive and benefit from the freedom that would bring. While some took part-time teaching jobs, women's main obligations were at home. Women cooked for each other and supported one another with their ever-growing families. At *shabbos* dinners they sat at the opposite end of the table to the men and served them first. Girls and boys didn't attend each other's birthday parties and even at weddings they ate and danced separately. The obligation is upon women to set the tone; if men stray, it is because women have overstepped, into their space.

So, at twelve, I celebrated my bas mitzvah, my coming of age into Jewish womanhood. My brothers' bar mitzvahs, at thirteen, had been held in the *shul* hall and took place over a whole weekend, with guests travelling from across the country. Bar mitzvahs mattered hugely in our community but bas mitzvah parties, my mother told me, were for secular girls who had something to prove and not for people like us. Attracting attention to a girl once she was 'of age' was inappropriate and Charedi families gave no great sense of occasion to female maturation. We certainly hadn't celebrated it for my sisters, so I was surprised, but pleased, when Mummy suggested a small gathering for mine. It felt as though she was shining her light on me, that she knew me and what I might like, just a little. In contrast to my brothers' celebrations, it was an extremely modest affair. We invited six girls – classmates and friends from the Jewish youth group – to my dining room, where we ate potato latkes and I was presented with a prayer book with my name inscribed in gilt on its brown jacket. It was the first time my mother took me to a shop to choose an outfit that wasn't a hand-me-down and I picked out a skirt, mid-calf-length, with flowers printed in shades of grey, and a matching square-cut blouse that I left untucked to feel like a jacket. Sitting at the table with my friends should have filled me with pride but I felt dread at the thought of how much more responsibility I'd have to carry in my 'adult' life.

I would soon learn that, more than anything, my bas mitzvah marked my retreat from the public gaze. It was confirmation of my place as a woman in the eyes of G-d and with it came the expectation that I would assume my prescribed feminine role with quiet strength and resilience. Like my older sisters, I would no longer sing at our table, I would pray consistently, and always cover my elbows and knees. Everything so far had been practice. Now, I would be judged for each infraction.

According to my mother, this was when the real religious work began. It was time to become more mature – a little woman taking her next steps towards her life's purpose: marriage and babies. I had to learn to curb my enthusiasm for the world and stop drawing attention to myself, though I never stopped longing to do so.

Up until this point, I hadn't been permitted to participate in fasting on the six religious fast days that mark out and commemorate centuries-old Jewish tragedies. I would watch my older siblings give up food and water for a day, envious of an experience that I wasn't privy to. Now, finally, I, too, would get to deprive myself in order to transcend my physical body and bring myself closer to G-d. I had been allowed three practice fasts in the year before my bas mitzvah and I hadn't tried to cheat in any of them. Where some may have resented the practice, instead this grown-up act excited me.

Coming of age also came with an invitation into my mother's secret woman's world, a world in which she called bras 'spectacles' and sanitary pads 'supplies' to shield the men around us from the very idea of female bodies. I was expected to help more around the house, which entailed endless dishwashing, serving guests, peeling potatoes and other drudgery that furthered me on my path to being a perfect wife and mother. Though I had no interest in domesticity, it all felt worth it to be welcomed into my mother's inner circle. I became her right hand, trusted to answer the phone to the brides and other women who called with messages for the rabbi's wife. Mummy held monthly get-togethers for women in the community and she began asking me to join. I usually stayed in the kitchen with Devorah, eating snacks that the *shul* paid for, but Mummy's occasional offer for me to sit alongside her was even more delicious.

Though I tried my best to meet my new religious responsibilities, I still struggled to suppress the disquiet that had been bubbling within me ever since that first bite of challah with unwashed hands. Throughout my childhood I felt like I was playing hide-and-seek with both my mother and G-d, simultaneously hiding my transgressions and longing for them to catch me. I continued to fake my daily prayers and pretended I'd washed my hands whenever I knew I could get away with it. On *shabbos*, in synagogue, I'd sit beside my mother, following the service in my book of the Old Testament with my right forefinger while using my left to find explicit mentions of anything rude and vulgar – of which there were plenty.

I had learned through my private tests that I had my own relationship with G-d, independent of the rules and independent of my parents' expectations. By the time I turned twelve, I had realized that G-d's disapproval and my mother's disapproval were two very different things, and G-d's was not the one I feared.

My belief in G-d's existence was never in question. In fact, it was because of my belief in Him that I worked so hard to find the truth behind all of the rules that stood between us. At school, I'd get sent home for arguing against my teachers' interpretations of the Bible. My parents would sigh when they'd see me walk through the front door in the middle of the day. They were less bothered by the fact that I had an opinion than the fact that I continued to voice it out loud.

'I'm going to give you a little notebook and you can write down all the things you want to say and ask me afterwards,' my mother said. I didn't bother with that because I didn't expect any more answers from her than I did the teachers.

At home, there was a bookshelf in the dining room, a little deeper than the others, where I'd run my hand along the spines of the heavy, leather-bound religious texts wondering if they contained the answers to my theological questions. I really wanted to read the damn things but, as a girl, I was prohibited. Besides, no one would bother to teach me to read

Aramaic. We did, however, have some books in English that my mother used to teach from, so I'd pick up *The River, the Kettle and the Bird: A Torah Guide to Successful Marriage* or a pamphlet about the weekly Torah portion and search them for answers instead. The contents only furthered my confusion. Everything about our belief system was being sold to me as definitive, but I had already found out for myself that it was about what my parents and teachers wanted of me, not what G-d did. This was another paradox of my young life that frustrated me.

The other girls around me were experiencing similar graduations into their teenage years but they weren't questioning G-d in the same way. The Private Conversation Club had changed its name to the more demure Cliquely Activities. We had chants and a dance that we carefully choreographed but the other girls had become wary of straying too close to topics deemed inappropriate by our families. I grew tired of not being able to tell them what I was really thinking and slowly lost interest in their company. The truth was, as much as I needed friendship, there weren't other people like me in my social circles. It felt like I was a lone lamb questioning the rest of the flock.

My only real friend was Dina. She was small with big, beautiful lips, blue eyes, milky-white skin dotted with freckles and short, bobbed, brown hair. She was sharp-witted but reserved and she fascinated me. We'd been put in a class together at school and I sensed, in part from the time she taught me how to shrink a crisp packet in the oven, that her mother's permitted activities and topics of conversation were more relaxed than mine. She was one of the only people I could speak with in the candid way I loved. She dispelled taboos for me and normalized things that I'd been taught to be embarrassed about. When I was on my period at her house, which I had been taught to treat with a sense of shame, she made light of me trying to hide it from her. She'd suggest we go for walks along the stream at the end of her road and the concept of doing things for no purpose other than enjoyment was mind-blowing to me. On weekends and after school, we'd hang out at each other's homes, experimenting in the kitchen or lying on our beds chatting about our small worlds. Dina grew to be my best friend but I found that, through the warmth of our friendship, I enjoyed any opportunity to feel physically close to her, too, like when she asked to hold hands or help her unhook her earrings from her hair, which was frequently.

On one of these occasions, some weeks after my bas mitzvah, we were lying in my brothers' room, on the bed, and decided we should practise for when we kissed boys – no tongues of course. I'm not sure who suggested it. It may well have been me. That brief press of her lips against mine was electric. She pulled away but I lingered for too long, my eyes darting across her face to her mouth with optimism. I had no idea that this moment offered a crystal ball's gaze into who I really was. I didn't know yet that this version of a woman existed. I expected to marry a man and accepted it as fact, in the same way as I knew the sky was blue. It would be years before I could begin to truly question my pre-ordained path.

As it is for all teenagers, growing up allowed my world to expand. Although for me this was in far smaller measure, I revelled in every new opportunity that came my way.

One of the changes I'd most anticipated came the summer after my bas mitzvah. Being of age meant that I was allowed to go to summer camp for the first time. Summer camp was the stuff of legend – a place where teenage girls from Charedi communities across the UK could spend two weeks hanging out with the extra freedom that came from shirking responsibilities and the restrictions that came with protecting us from the male gaze. For parents, it was a kosher way to keep us entertained. To girls, this ring-fenced freedom was important socially, and it was relished. And it was where all the cool girls went.

The camp took place in a boarding school in Montrose, Scotland, and the only male was a visiting rabbi who wore a baseball cap instead of his black hat to indicate he was in 'fun' mode. Every morning, he led prayers, and then waved a cheery goodbye, leaving us in a man-free zone. We would wait for the big, heavy doors to click shut and erupt into jubilant cheers and songs as we made a start to our day. We played team games and chanted on the tabletops. For all of us, it was the only time in the year we could enjoy a big, communal space only for women, and it was completely liberating. The head counsellor was an eighteen-year-old called Ahuva, who was the most beautiful woman I had ever seen. I wanted to spend all my time next to her and bask in her glory, oblivious at the time as to why. In this new place, I felt I could inhabit myself in a way I'd never been able to before, yet I still didn't quite know how to insert myself into this new world.

In Glasgow, I was the rabbi's daughter. I had inherited my mother's superiority complex and therefore sat comfortably in my place as part of an influential family. Here, however, I was a small-town girl from a tiny community. I was suddenly among girls who came from large, thriving Jewish communities in

Manchester and London, and who had never heard of my father, or the synagogue I was so proud of. They had cooler, more expensive clothes than me and their parents sent food parcels to them twice each week, where mine sent none. I had a new-found sense of my place in the world and I wasn't sure I liked it. Even in my liberation, I was still somehow an outsider.

My only saving grace was Penina, a girl who sought me out on the first day because our brothers were friends. She invited me to her dorm room, where she had stacks of food squirrelled away and a mobile phone that she used to call into radio stations, requesting them to play songs for some boy in London. This absolutely blew my mind – a whole new dimension of naughty things I could do that shocked and thrilled me beyond measure.

When I went home to Glasgow, I would call Penina on her mobile from my parents' landline, hoping they wouldn't notice their inflated phone bill. I searched out my father's old pager in a drawer and clipped it to my skirt waistband, giving only Penina the number so that she could reach me. My world was a little bigger again and Penina would become one of my closest confidants.

The early years of my adolescence had brought both good and bad. Though I loved this proximity to adulthood and the world my parents inhabited, the more I learned, the more I came up against the boundaries of my existence. Every taste of the wider world left me feeling more boxed in than ever. Even at the furthest reaches of my community, I had yet to feel like I really belonged. Little did I know that, within a couple of years, I would find myself somewhere where I'd feel more alienated than ever.

3

Anthrax

שׁוּחָה עֲמֻקָּה פִּי זָרוֹת זְעוּם יְהוָה יִפָּל שָׁם

The mouth of a forbidden woman is a deep pit; he who is doomed by the Lord falls into it.

Proverbs 22:14

WE LANDED AT BEN GURION Airport, Tel Aviv, the day before my fourteenth birthday and the pretty blonde passport officer with a tanned complexion looked down from her desk to congratulate me.

'*Mazel tov*, Yehudit,' she said in a cascading accent with emphatic syllables that gave my name a new, harsher ending.

It was August 2001, and Mummy and Daddy had taken Devorah and me to start a new life in Israel. By then, my older siblings were all married or studying away from home so they already felt somewhat distant. Now, it would just be the four of us. Tel Aviv, where we'd landed, was secular but our new life was to be within a community more strict than any in the UK. Emigration to the holy land is called *aliyah*, which translates as 'upwards', and we'd moved from unholy but green Glasgow to the lofty, brown Judean Hills where the Middle Eastern sun was strong and I, the rabbi's daughter, was suddenly the least religious girl for miles around. I was hopeful that this was my chance to discard my out-of-towner status and integrate into a bigger Jewish community in a way that I hadn't managed to at summer camp.

As we settled in, one of our first tasks was to go and collect our gas masks, a necessary mundanity for civilians in a country used to war. As we stood in line, my mother distanced herself from me. 'Your collarbone is showing. I am ashamed to stand next to you,' she chastised, and stepped away, crying. I was confused. I was wearing an entirely modest long-sleeved top that was deemed perfectly acceptable no more than twenty-four hours ago. We were in Israel now, the holy land. The stakes were higher, rules tighter – in this community, at least – but no one had explained what that would look like. It daunted me because it daunted my mother, so I felt utterly unassured about what life had in store for me now.

The endless and bafflingly specific rules irritated me almost immediately. I wasn't allowed to wear hoodies or tops with slogans or brands on them. My clothes had to be made of thicker, woven fabrics so as not to hint at a curve or the location of a nipple. Where cream woollen tights from Tesco were a marker of modesty in Glasgow, in our new neighbourhood within Beit Shemesh, a crowded city that spilled down the hillsides west of Jerusalem, only thick nude tights or long, opaque, knee-length stockings, worn high above my hemline, were deemed conservative enough. I wore my hair in a long, chaste braid down my back during the week but I wasn't allowed to braid it on *shabbos* because it's considered 'building work.'

My parents thought that making *aliyah* was a wonderful favour to us children. My father believed that every step we took in the holy land was a merit earned for 'The World to Come.' But this promise came without any acknowledgement of how hard it was going to be in a new place and a proper school for the first time. We would be speaking Hebrew, a language I'd written and read my whole life but of which I had no conversational, working knowledge. To make matters worse, neither did my mother, which limited the ways in which she could support me. I had grown up speaking English and understood a little Yiddish from my stays with Miriam, which had at least some currency in my new neighbourhood, but without Hebrew I struggled to communicate, let alone with any depth. I tried to keep in touch with my friends back home using the fax machine that we stored on our apartment's enclosed balcony, snacking on the familiarity of hearing from people I knew in a language I understood. But away from the bustle of my family home, with visitors regularly crossing our threshold, I soon found myself feeling lonely.

My parents chose Israeli schools for us instead of the international one for foreigners, so I was placed in a high school class of thirty girls, none of whom I could hold a meaningful conversation with. I didn't know how to hang out with these girls who played skipping at break time and seemed more suspended in childhood than I was. I considered myself an adult at the grand age of fourteen, and their innocence bored me. Instead, I passed most of my spare time alone, sitting at my desk, doodling or people-watching, intrigued by but not included in their cliques. After so long at the tiny school above the *shul*, I was overwhelmed by the huge campus I found impossible to navigate, and I had never had a timetable before, nor had to remember different books for different classes. I felt like I was always turning up at the wrong place, at the wrong time, with the wrong equipment. My inability to assimilate disappointed me. I was finally in this bigger world but I couldn't find my way around it and no one would show me how.

Devorah, by contrast, was ten, impressionable and much less cynical than I was. She was in a primary school down the road, with more English speakers, and adapted more willingly. Within weeks she had made a friend and asked my mother to dress her the same as the other girls, in patterned white tights with blue leather shoes with decorative cut-outs and a navy skirt.

The curriculum was a state one, meaning there was secular as well as religious education. My *shul* education had focused on the religious aspects so my new classmates were much further along in subjects like maths and biology than I was and I checked out of lessons entirely, unable to follow the classes. The only lesson I enjoyed was English For English Speakers, which I had once a week. It was the one time at school when I could participate. Outside school, I was sent to a tutor weekly, a young, newly married woman who spoke English with an American accent and whose job was to bring me up to speed with my schoolwork. Of course, without any guidance, I never managed to bring the right books back from school so we'd chat instead, in whatever rudimentary

Hebrew I could muster, mostly slang. Though we weren't getting any work done, I liked having someone to talk to. It was the only time in my new life in Israel when I felt like I had something that slightly resembled companionship. Even at home I felt isolated, and family tensions there were growing by the day.

Since arriving in Israel, we were all at odds with one another. My father was high on the heady blend of religious spiritualism and hot weather but he was clueless about how things worked there so he frequently missed paying the bills, meaning the phone or electric supply would sporadically be cut off. Mummy, on the other hand, had never really wanted to leave Glasgow in the first place. Without anyone to see, or a community to tend to, she would go for days without leaving the house. My eldest brother, Dov Ber, was living in Jerusalem with his wife and baby, and we'd often go to them for *shabbos*, but it was clear that my mother struggled with her status at these gatherings. She'd gone from being a leader in the community, hosting large meals and earning the respect and quiet admiration of other women, to being a foreigner who didn't speak the language or have anything to get up for in the morning except Devorah and me. We weren't enough, and Mummy didn't have the capacity to navigate my needs as well as her own. In her own quest to survive this new life, I constantly felt like she was leaving me behind.

My parents argued frequently about being there, and while my mother was distracted and unmoored by her new position in the world, I was left to put on the laundry and make cottage cheese sandwiches to sustain my sister and me. In addition to my own uncertainty about my place in the world, financially sands felt like they were shifting, too. For the first time ever, we'd go out to restaurants for pizza and I had new clothes that weren't hand-me-downs, yet the next week the power would go down at home. There seemed no pattern to what we could or couldn't afford, which created a sense of chaos. All of this insecurity began to mount, and as always no one explained anything to me, so I was left feeling anxious at all times. Tension lived in our home like an uninvited guest who was taking up more and more space. Nothing was going well and nowhere felt stable.

At school, I was bored and enforced my own isolation to hold on to my identity. I decided that if I wasn't going to be able to integrate, it was better to stop trying than to fail or, worse, be rejected by people who didn't want to be my friends. Only accounting for myself gave me a sense of control. Meanwhile, Devorah was progressing at school, picking up the language, joining in with lessons and making friends, which I found especially irritating. Rather than feeling envious of her, I was disparaging. It wasn't her fault, but she had abandoned me by diving into this new life so easily.

Summer temperatures routinely hit thirty degrees Celsius in Beit Shemesh and one searingly hot late September afternoon I was sitting in our classroom, which was housed in a residential building, writing down a serial of my life so far for the girls around me. If I hadn't been so standoffish, this could have been a chance to make friends. As things were, it was just a way to pass the time. The two or three of them who spoke a little English were passing around the scraps of paper as I scribbled installations; flitting around desks in what was essentially a living room were thirty girls wearing long, navy-blue, pleated skirts, thick-woven cotton shirts and nude tights. Our teacher, Mrs Feldman, was 5ft 9 with broad shoulders, wide hips and a stiff brown wig. She had, I believe, thirteen children, including one who was only six weeks old at the time, and she wore a straight, dark-green skirt suit that buttoned up to the collar and always smelled of sweat. She would speak to me in Yiddish and I had, until now, felt a motherliness from her that comforted me.

My not-modest-enough family and my inability to understand Hebrew – which had now morphed into my stubborn belief that I never would – meant I was already unpopular with the teachers and today this didn't help matters. As Mrs Feldman caught sight of my pieces of paper making their way around, she called to every girl to sit down and walked to the front of her desk, leaning her ample bottom on its edge. She spoke, in Hebrew, slowly and clearly enough for me to understand.

'There is one girl here who is like anthrax for the rest of the class,' she said, before launching into a speech about bad influences and being wary of who you spent time with after school. She never mentioned my name but she didn't need to. Everyone turned to look, their faces full of judgement. I felt confused and betrayed, by the classmates who'd buoyed me on to write down my story and by the teacher I had trusted as one of my only safety nets. She embarrassed me and it hurt. I wanted the earth to swallow me up. It was at this moment I realized there was no chance of me succeeding there.

During our first winter holiday, we took a trip back to the UK for my brother Shmuel's wedding. When I returned to school, the secretary – a seventeen-year-old married girl who wore a wig and pillbox hat – handed me two brown envelopes addressed to my parents. One congratulated us on my brother's wedding, the other called us in for a meeting with the principal. It seemed we had been tripped up by another unwritten rule, in an already cryptic society that my parents hadn't yet got to grips with. Students were not allowed to expose themselves to the impurities of the outside world by leaving the holy land without the school's permission. Life in our community was always balanced on a knife edge, threatening to tip over at the smallest infraction. Arbitrary rules like this one were a way of maintaining decorum within the community and controlling the population. The headmaster asked me to leave the school for travelling outside of Israel without permission; he'd just as soon have asked me to leave if my father had stopped wearing the correct, wide-brimmed Borsalino hat.

It served as a harsh reality check for my parents. It was also deeply embarrassing to them. Although none of these choices had been mine, in Israel my parents and, by extension, the community (or perhaps it was the other way around), now earmarked me as a problem child.

My despairing mother and father eagerly searched for the wisdom to deal with this mess and took me to see a revered English-speaking rabbi. He had a tiny frame but famously wore 120 tasselled prayer vests, *tzitzis*, one on top of another, which gave him the appearance of an overstuffed fairground prize. I had never been in front of a man this holy before and I was in awe. My parents presented me to him as their daughter, a bit of a tearaway whose neckline was sometimes a bit low, which told me all I needed to know about their motivation for taking me there. 'G-d watches over fools,' he told my parents, without looking at me. I looked at my shoes.

Until that moment, I had been sure that godliness and goodness went hand in hand and I was certain that wasn't what G-d thought of me. G-d knew me and I wasn't a fool. But the rabbi's words wiped out my idea of what holiness looked like – his dismissal was cruel, and surely he was no closer to G-d than I was – and I didn't have anything to replace it with. Perhaps my relationship with G-d wasn't as mutual as I had thought. Perhaps I was just a fool, after all. If my parents left any wiser, I didn't. I only felt more isolated.

To make matters worse, my new place of education was to be a school set up for girls who'd been thrown out of other schools, in the occupied territories of East Jerusalem, a two-hour bus ride away. It was the height of the Second Intifada and I had to change buses at a terminal in the settlement of French Hill, known for its uprisings and fighting. Those long journeys were filled with fear of the very real threat of kidnappings. Each morning my mother would cry: 'I don't know if you're going to come back alive.' Her fear weighed heavily on me at all times. I was carrying her emotions and no one was carrying mine.

The new school was situated inside a purpose-built community centre and was much smaller than the last. It was punctuated with outdoor spaces, meaning we often took lessons outside the classroom. There was no mistaking that this was a place for dropouts and we were reminded of it often, not least by the presence, next door, of a high-achieving school for girls whose pupils turned one way at the bus stop while we turned the other. The problem with going to a school for dropouts is there's an inclination to live up to your name. Many of the girls in my class of ten, including me, found it hard to shake off the label during our time there. Nonetheless, the teachers were kind and made an effort to do things differently for kids who hadn't made the grade at their previous schools. We wore white ribbed knee-socks, which was a whole new category of immodest for me. I had already been dismissed as naughty, despite having done nothing out of line, and my new-found autonomy on the long journey to school gave me an opportunity to further play the part, so I decided I may as well. Three days in, I bought two pairs of socks, one red-and-orange-striped and one with blue stripes. While waiting between buses I swapped my school socks for these new, funky ones. This started a bit of a trend, which I was proud of. It cemented my social status at school where I was otherwise seen as a bit of a nerd who spoke English with a 'proper' English accent, in contrast to the others' American twang. What with my trend-setting socks and the bootleg Avril Lavigne cassettes I'd buy in the bus station market, everyone wanted to become my friend. I had a new, interested audience, and for the first time felt like I might have a community of my own. To top it all off I had a massive crush – that I didn't know was a crush – on one of the only two girls who didn't fangirl over me. Peri was American, short but perfectly formed with caramel-licked skin and glossy black hair like Courteney Cox in *Friends*. She exuded sexuality and thought nothing of pulling her shirt back over her shoulders, leaning forward over her desk and asking, in Hebrew: 'Rabbi, do you think I've tanned?'

Being there, away from the intensity of our new community in Beit Shemesh, opened my mind. These girls wore immodest short sleeves, form-fitting long denim skirts and unconservative chunky Skechers shoes. I didn't have any of those clothes but I used my babysitting money – from looking after our neighbours' kids – to accumulate a secret wardrobe of my own. I didn't copy what they wore but enjoyed a new-found thrill in buying equally immodest things I liked the look of at the mall; things that reflected my own tastes. This invited constant arguments with my mother. Every time she found something new at home or spotted me leaving the house in an unacceptable outfit, she'd yell at me. The old me would have feared her disapproval but I loved those clothes, and I loved how they made me feel. They gave me power and legitimacy in myself.

As my independence grew, my relationship with my mother started to reach breaking point. Our roles had shifted and I'd belittle her frequently. 'Mummy's not done any washing,' I'd tell Daddy when he walked in, offloading my resentment towards her on a daily basis. At the same time, my mother's growing bitterness about being there was clashing with my father's perpetual optimism. I exploited their frustration in a bid to get them both to notice me. Even their disapproval would count as care.

'The milk here tastes weird,' I'd say.

'But aren't the yoghurts lovely?' Daddy would counter.

'They're awful,' Mummy would snap back. 'Full of sugar.'

Everything jarred. And there was nothing any of us could do to alleviate it. I was so miserable that I was barely eating. I'd manage one meal a day at most. Mummy noticed and started making us sandwiches again but it felt like too little, too late; I couldn't shift my anger towards her and always threw them in the bin. The more I expressed myself, the more reactive and defensive Mummy became. She got stricter, too. She wanted to know at all times what I was doing and what I was reading. After a life of being able to fly under the radar, I felt like she was cutting me down to size.

I spent an increasing amount of time in the basement of our apartment building, where my parents kept a box of journals on Jewish thought. I'd flick through them in a desperate search for answers to the impossible situation I was living in. On one occasion, when she caught me, she shouted down, 'What are you doing down there? Are you trying to go off the *derech*?', invoking a concept known in religious Jewish circles as 'OTD', the act of leaving this most religious life. She was goading me.

Funnily enough, I had found one issue that offered rabbinical advice to parents whose kids were at risk of exactly that. I found myself compelled to read it and would often go down to revisit its pages even though I knew my religion was never something I wanted to leave behind.

For the first time, though, the security of G-d felt like it was slipping away. School was getting better, friends and teachers continued to foster a warm environment in which faith could be questioned a little more easily (we were already naughty, so their only job now was to keep us religious). This sat at odds with home, however, where my curiosity continued to be met with silence. I was tired and confused from all the grappling. The more dilemmas or degradations I faced for doing nothing wrong, the more the unanswered questions piled up. I began to wonder: if every answer failed to satisfy me, maybe it was my faith that was wrong, not me? But I couldn't afford not to believe. I never wanted to stop. G-d was the only person who loved me and I didn't want to lose Him.

I was colouring outside the lines but my mother couldn't grasp that none of my minor acts of rebellion were about my core beliefs. I just wanted autonomy and to be noticed – by anyone. I wanted the opportunity to grow into my own person. My mother's constant barbs hurt me to the point that we otherwise barely spoke. One night, after she'd gone to bed, I decided to speak to Daddy. I sat in my mother's rocking chair trying to explain that the boundaries I was pushing at weren't about G-d; it was the systems – and rabbis – that I couldn't stand.

'It's not that I don't believe. It's that I don't respect men with beards and black coats,' I remember saying. To me, their clothes didn't automatically earn respect and their rules didn't stack up. I'd tested them enough to know that. This must have offended Daddy because to him I was attacking exactly who he was. He sighed, or maybe cried. I looked away because I didn't want to see that I'd hurt him, to face my own behaviour.

I'd felt bold standing up for my opinions in our living room, but in my bedroom the bravado fell away and I felt desperately, desperately alone. I was ashamed that I'd embarrassed him and I felt I'd let myself down. It was Mummy who dished out barbs; I didn't do that.

I was adrift. How could I navigate this world with no map? I began to wonder if the next world would be easier.

The next day's argument with my mother was about a school

bowling trip that evening, which she wouldn't give me money to pay for.

'I don't trust you,' she shouted. 'I don't believe you're going where you say.'

Refusing to give up the prospect of a rare pleasant night out, I left the house and took my babysitting money with me instead.

When I got to the bowling alley and called her from a friend's phone to let her know I was OK, she could hear voices in the background.

'What are you doing? Are you with boys?' she interrogated.

There were no boys. Still, I felt guilty. I knew she was worried and would be getting more and more hysterical as the night wore on. I left my friends and got the next bus home, imagining she would be relieved to see me and maybe even have something warm to say for once. But when the bus pulled into my street and I opened our front door, Mummy wasn't there. The flat was empty and dark. No one was there to comfort me or tell me everything would be OK. No one was pacing the hallway, anxious for my return. At this point I would've taken a scolding gladly if it meant someone was at least concerned for my well-being. I didn't think it was possible to feel more alone, more done with everything, less understood, but I did. This cycle of vying for love and attention and receiving none had become relentless. I wanted an exit.

I reached into the fridge for a half-drunk bottle of flat lemon Fanta, then took a packet of ibuprofen from the drawer in the kitchen counter. I didn't bother turning on the light. I'd never before considered how I would go through with this, but now it felt surprisingly clinical. This was the obvious answer. I sat myself down at the square laminate table and began mechanically popping the pills from their blister pack. I felt entirely numb. I took a swig from the bottle, threw a handful of painkillers into my mouth and washed them down. Then another handful. And another. I must have swallowed forty-five pills. I had no idea that ibuprofen wouldn't kill me; it was simply the first thing I found. It was as if I was on autopilot.

As I waited for the pills to take their effect, I called a rabbi who I sometimes turned to for advice and told him: 'Thank you, but this is what's about to happen to me now.' I was trying to say goodbye but, as a responsible adult, obviously he called the police.

I was huddled up and shaking, thinking I was on my way to death, when, from our dark kitchen, three floors up, I saw the flashing blue-and-red lights of emergency vehicles cast against the walls. Within moments there was banging on the apartment door and a voice I didn't know bellowing my name. I didn't answer.

In Israel doors are bomb-proof, so they had no choice but to drill through the cement frame. The whole flat shook, until a figure in police uniform, a blue shirt with navy lapels, appeared in the hole left by the door. I grabbed a penknife.

'Don't come closer or I'll slit my wrists,' I howled.

He looked at the empty blister packs.

'Listen,' he said. 'That's not going to kill you but you need to go to hospital or you're going to have terrible tummy ache.'

I could hear my words echoing back to me inside my head. I felt exposed and angry. My plan hadn't worked and now I felt humiliated. I was melting, physically and emotionally.

When he got me downstairs, into the night, I saw that my parents were waiting on the pavement. How long had they been there? I wondered why they hadn't bothered to intervene. Why weren't they saying anything to me? Even when my life was on the line, I still couldn't get them to care. The policeman put me in the back of an ambulance and they followed in their car to Hadassah Medical Center. I was taken to the emergency department and given a charcoal liquid in a disposable cup by a nurse who watched me drink the whole thing before asking when I'd last eaten. I hadn't eaten since the day before. They kept me in overnight.

The next morning, my parents and I sat around a table in a hospital side room with a social worker. My mother was crying. I was mortified by her ineptitude. The social worker was secular and seemed unsure of whose toes or which rules she was stepping on with each question she asked us. She asked for instances of what had caused me to attempt suicide and whether home was dysfunctional. I looked around at another tableful of adults who couldn't offer me protection and realized I needed help. My parents couldn't, or wouldn't, give it to me; I heard them telling the social worker there was no way they could look after me. I was shocked by how readily they abandoned me. Even after fifteen years of vying for their love and attention and not getting what I needed in return, I still couldn't believe that they would let me go so easily. It felt like they weren't even trying. I was admitted to a mental health ward at the hospital, where I'd stay for the next six weeks.

The ward was long with heavy swing-doors and shared bedrooms off to the sides. There were also three inoffensive social rooms for group sessions: one with a table and chairs for crafts, a day room with a library and cuboid couches in royal blue, and a smaller room for quiet conversation. It was a dumping ground for kids with all manner of unrelated problems. One girl had been raped, there was a boy detoxing from drugs, a girl who obsessively drank so much water she was damaging her body, and others who had eating disorders. I was on suicide watch, so I couldn't shower or go to the loo without an adult. The staff were all secular and they were empathetic towards me. They had seen plenty of children from my background before and as they saw it there were two things wrong with me: the first was that my parents were too religious to handle me and I was quite clearly distressed by their expectations; the second was that all my picking at meals and binning sandwiches had left me thinner than the adults thought I should be. When Mummy and Daddy turned up for meetings, I refused to speak to them and no one pushed it. They didn't come to see me other than that. It felt like they'd finally given up on me.

One week, frustrated by my silence, my mother came in to collect my dirty laundry. 'Yehudis Gittel,' she shouted across the ward. 'There's not enough dirty knickers in here.'

'Just take the bag,' the nurse told her.

She could never shout 'I love you' but she could humiliate me in a crowded room with ease.

Once again, I was utterly alone with no idea what was going to happen next or how long I'd be there. Each day was the same: meals in the day room interspersed with group sessions, crafts (usually threading beads) and journaling with a teacher who came in every morning to keep us up to speed with our writing. Every child on the ward had to attend daily weigh-ins. I made myself act tough to get through the routine, but at night I went to sleep with a sharp shard of thick acrylic that I'd taken during a craft session. I'd clutch it under my pillow, believing that if it all got too much I could use it to kill myself. The possibility of escape offered me comfort.

I struck up a friendship with Nasreen, a girl from East Jerusalem a little older than me, who had anorexia. It was the first time I'd been free to have a conversation with a Muslim person. She came from a religious family and struggled with the expectations they had for her, just as I did. She told me that when her brother visited her in intensive care, he slapped her around the face for not wearing hijab, so she couldn't go home, either. Nasreen and I would do each other's eyebrows and my room-mate Shoshana taught me songs from Israeli television. There was a boy called Dvir who would pull up a chair to chat when I got into bed each night and wrote me a love letter that confused me no end, given that the concept of boyfriends was totally alien to me. I also befriended a nurse from Glasgow, who occasionally took me outside and gave me a cigarette, and a student medic in his early twenties, who would take me for a can of Coke and a walk around the hospital corridors, until he got found out.

Bizarrely, it was on that ward where I found a camaraderie I'd not yet felt in Israel. It was the first time that a whole group of adults had tended to me and the first time I felt the comfort of others' investment in what happened to me. It didn't really matter to me whether they got it right or wrong – I enjoyed being treated like a teenager, with teenager's problems, rather than a little sinful adult.

It was a kind of formative time – ridiculous and awful in equal measure but, in the context of what had been going on at home, a reprieve. I wasn't allowed to die, so I just had to wait for what happened next. I had no idea it would only move me further away from my family.

It was decided that home was no good for me – and vice versa – so social services, with my parents' permission, agreed that I should live with a foster family across the city. The couple were in their thirties, a respected family who were essentially running a children's factory, taking money off both the state and the parents of the kids in their care, to keep us under their roof. They lived in a flat filled with their own children. Through a door that kept us locked out of their home but free to run feral in our own, was another flat where eleven misfits, now including me, slept on a collection of mattresses and narrow metal cots across the stone-tiled floors of three bedrooms. The walls and rooms were bare and the whole place smelled of old sweat. There was a kitchen with paper plates, disposable cups and a packet of breast pads, presumably left by a teenage mum who'd lived there some time before me. I made use of them and stuffed two in each side of my bra to enhance my flat chest.

We rarely saw the foster parents. At lunchtime, they would leave a tray outside our door containing a few chewy, greasy chicken schnitzels to share. There was only enough for a few bites each and I was always starving. My family were in only occasional contact via the house phone and I remember Mummy bringing Devorah to see me, while she waited outside crying in the Jerusalem rain. My father sent the foster family money to buy me clothes, which he would have been furious to know I used to buy my first pairs of trousers: two pairs of jeans, one straight-legged and one so baggy that they covered my new chunky Skechers. I had no idea how the sizes worked but I muddled through the rails with a friend until I settled on the right fit. I loved the way I looked in the changing-room mirror; how unrestricted my legs felt. I could move and run and I delighted in that feeling. For the first time, I was resolute in my decision to break the rules. All the instability around me had returned me to the security in the one thing I knew: G-d and my relationship with Him. The adults had all fucked off but He loved me anyway. The jeans became my uniform, worn with a fringed head scarf around the waist as my nod to modesty when I went into town with friends. I enjoyed creating these new standards for myself – a Charedi girl who decided which part of the rules worked for me. I moved the goalposts and finally got a taste of what it was to have agency over my decisions. G-d didn't seem to mind.

I was finally happy with people my age and I had accumulated a small group of friends, some leftover from school, some from the street. We passed time together talking, smoking cigarettes that we bought individually from a cup on the newsagent's counter, and chomping and spitting our way through bags of roasted sunflower seeds bought from the market. We got piercings together, too, in a filthy back-alley shop, which seemed to be a pastime for kids in the city. Four steel studs dotted my left ear, two in my right. My mother would have been furious, not least because the Torah forbids deliberate wounding.

School had got rid of me after the Fanta and pills, so there wasn't much else to do.

'They're not a school for girls who want to commit suicide,' the foster parents told me.

My father would get in touch with me on practical matters – such as bringing clothes and money from home – via text message. There was never any offer of tenderness. No reminder that they loved me or a plea for me to come home. Despite a life that would suggest otherwise, I spent every moment waiting for it. But I still refused to talk to them in person – not that they ever tried.

I don't know whether it was my parents or the social worker who offered up my next move but, six weeks later, it was suggested to me that my best option would be to go back to the UK and be schooled in England. Within a week of my father telling me this plan, I was on a plane home. In all that time, I had never returned to our family apartment in Israel, never packed up my room. Instead, my father sent a purple holdall on wheels into which I packed my jeans, Skechers and the few other items of clothing I had – the sum total of my possessions now.

I spent the night before I left walking, talking and smoking with friends. A few were old enough to drive the rest of us around. Like the desert, Jerusalem is bathed in heat in summer but freezing in winter. It was a February evening and we were cold. A friend hadn't made it home in time for curfew and her mother wouldn't let her in the house, so I'd stayed out with her in solidarity. We ended up in a valley on the outskirts of the city with two men in their twenties, one of whom she vaguely knew.

As they drove us back, I stared out of the window at this beautiful place that hadn't been able to take care of me. It was almost light, with a white light reflected off the sandy-coloured stones that were not yet warmed by sun. I picked up my purple holdall from the foster flat and let these two men I didn't know drive me on to the airport. I don't recall the flight back to England at all but I recall what happened after I arrived.

4

Make yourself useful

אַל־תִּתְחַר בַּמְּרֵעִים אַל־תְּקַנֵּא בְּעֹשֵׂי עַוְלָה

Do not be vexed by evil men; do not be incensed by wrongdoers.

Psalms 37:1

ONCE AGAIN, I FOUND MYSELF somewhere that wasn't home. Manchester was a city I'd only visited with family, to stay with my grandmas or to see my brother who had been studying in a yeshiva – a boys' seminary – there.

The Charedi community there lived in the north of the city, where polluted, populated A-roads stretched three miles from its metropolitan centre, past the prison and into suburbs dense with first- and second-generation immigrants. There was a grid of roads occupied almost exclusively by religious Jewish families who were served by local synagogues, kosher shops and faith schools, giving them no need to explore or socialize beyond the boundaries of their community.

I was fifteen now and sent to a small school for girls that was more secular than anything I'd encountered. Manchester's Jewish community was bigger than in Glasgow, which meant there were more layers of orthodoxy within it. With that came a wider choice of schools offering Jewish education, ranging from the type I'd been to when I was little, which was so religious it could barely be classed a school at all, to state-funded faith schools, like this one. It taught from the national curriculum as well as from Jewish texts and I was put to the bottom of the GCSE course with girls almost two years younger than me. I didn't really know what flew in those corridors and I became a bit of an exotic exhibit to the rest of the pupils, on account of arriving mid-year and with multiple ear-piercings. But to me, it was the school that felt exotic. I was suddenly exposed to new ideas. The girls lived in big houses with only one or two siblings, their parents were professionals, and they were on the path to university so I hoped I would be, too. Girls' education was valued here in a way I'd never experienced before. The girls invited me to the cinema with them at the weekend. I went to watch *8 Mile* three times just to soak up the experience of being there. There was routine and I had a uniform that, this time, in the familiarity of Britain, made me feel like I was a welcome part of something, rather than being forced to comply. I felt like I had been given back some joy, another shot at being a teenager, among people my own age who I could actually converse with. I was happy there.

My parents had arranged for me to stay with friends of theirs whose cavernous home had hosted us before, so it wasn't altogether unfamiliar. Everything there felt considered: their stripped-back floorboards were highly polished, they were vegetarian and never cooked with salt, and shoes were removed at the front door. I felt like clutter. I spent as much time as possible in my room so as not to get in their way. My grandmas both lived nearby, and I'd visit each of them weekly, but I felt like they were annoyed with me because of what had happened in Israel so I felt like clutter there too. I had to appear independent and capable to prove to them that I wasn't trouble, when really I just wanted someone to look after me.

My mother emailed occasionally, forwarding me articles or family news but never checking how I was. Her emails were always short and I'd reply with my tough-girl act.

'I'm fine,' I'd write, never acknowledging the hurt or things I found difficult. 'I've gone to Grandma for *shabbos*.' I never offered any more.

Daddy paid for my lodgings and sent me money to cover school lunches and my mobile phone, but he never contacted me.

I was completely unmoored. With no one taking responsibility for me, it felt as if there was nowhere I belonged. I'd been there for no more than three months when I went to stay with Miriam, who was now living in London, for the eight-day festival of *Pesach* (Passover) that April. *Pesach* marks the beginning of spring and commemorates the Jews' exodus from slavery in ancient Egypt. The rules around food are even stricter at *Pesach* than at any other time of year. Wheat products are forbidden, so Miriam cooked everything from scratch – even grinding almonds to make flour – and scrubbed the house from top to bottom to ensure not a crumb remained. I helped her with these tasks, taking the opportunity to tell her how unsettled I felt. She was upset to hear what I had to say. As the only person in the family who'd truly looked out for me, she still felt responsible for my happiness and said she'd help. I was just relieved that someone finally cared. Miriam had seen an advert in a community freesheet seeking a female lodger for a home ten minutes from my school. It was the home of a Jewish scholar, Todros Grynhaus, who had a large family of sons and daughters. She wrote down the number and, when I got back to Manchester, arranged for me to view the room. I took Rena, the daughter of a family we knew, who lived nearby and had instantly become a friend.

It was a box room with a single bed, wardrobe, desk, bedside table and a long, wavy mirror from Ikea tacked to the wall. It sat in an extension that they had built above the garage, which housed Todros's study. On our first meeting he was charismatic, gregarious even. He was about 6 ft tall and broad, with a tummy that was rounded but not quite fat. He was close to forty and wore the black trousers and white shirt of a Charedi man, the strings of his prayer vest hanging out, and black socks with leather open-toe sandals. His round face was covered by a short, blonde beard that grew a couple of inches off his chin, and his short hair was mostly covered by a black velvet skullcap, or *cappel.*

I didn't particularly like the room, which was so basic it looked like a prison cell. Rena's mother, who was a social worker, warned me against taking it.

'I can't tell you why,' she said. 'But take it from me: don't move in with them.'

Something about her warning made me feel uneasy, but I was desperate and without any other options. I wanted my own space and thought anything would be better than where I was. I stuffed my limited possessions back into my purple holdall and moved in a couple of days later.

Once installed, I covered my meagre wall space with fashion adverts I'd ripped out of *Glamour* magazine, a copy of which I'd pick up once a month on a Friday afternoon alongside a bag of mini Mars bars from Woolworths on the walk home from school.

The family was about as *frum* (observant) as mine. There were the same modesty rules and kosher kitchen, and the same segregation of the sexes – I spent time with the nine children as I would my own siblings. I addressed my host as 'rabbi', which was a secular and slightly obnoxious way to greet him on my part. I should have used his proper address, Rabbi Grynhaus – the accepted, honourable term for a scholar of his standing, despite him not actually being a clergyman – or better still not addressed him directly at all.

It was a busy, tense household with a forced cheeriness. I quickly learned that no one, including me, could show their true emotions. Todros was an authoritarian who punished his kids frequently, humiliating them for their mistakes or locking them in their bedroom for days at a time, but they weren't allowed to cry about it. His wife was a simpering woman who laughed too hard at his jokes and seemed indifferent to my presence. There was an edge in the air, always.

A couple of weeks after I arrived, I came home to find an array of new clothes, in my size, draped across my bed. I was still wearing my jeans, which they didn't approve of, so they'd chosen ones that were more *tznius* (modest) as their way of trying to impose their rules.

'I'm never going to wear this,' I said. 'You may as well take it all back.'

They could try to impose rules but I wasn't their child to punish if I broke them. The following Sunday we all piled into the car to Matalan to do just that.

Todros's wife and kids must have been browsing when he turned to me in the returns queue and asked, 'Do you need any bras?'

This, of course, was not only an inappropriate question for an older man to ask a young girl in any society but offended every law of modesty and suitable conversation between a man and woman, or girl, who was not his wife.

'Do you need any boxers?' I replied. Bravado was my default mask for discomfort.

He shushed me.

'That's not for you to ask,' I added.

Nothing more was said but a few weeks later he found me at the kitchen table, doing my homework, as I did most evenings. He stood beside me, the weight of his shadow looming over me, and offered me a cup of coffee. I'd never drunk coffee before.

'No, thank you,' I said. 'That's for adults.'

The kitchen was large and the table long enough to seat twelve. His wife was putting their younger children to bed.

'I'm having one,' he encouraged. 'Let me mix in some cocoa – it tastes sweet. You'll enjoy it.'

I nodded an 'OK', tempted now by his permission to try being an adult, and walked over to where he was standing.

The rich mix of bitter coffee granules and cheap chocolate powder was warming. It tasted good. I liked the ritual, the sophistication, even if drunk from an old mug faded by over-washing. I felt grown-up and respected.

From then on, Todros would come and find me there, alone, most nights and make coffee. I grew to feel nervous in his presence. Our conversation was always the same – awkward, superficial, always carried out standing up at the back of the kitchen. On milder nights, he'd take his coffee and have a cigarette on the bench outside. He'd ask me to sit with him but his body was big and the bench was small. I didn't want to occupy that space, touching or almost touching. I declined and stood back. Really, I would have liked to walk away with my coffee. Or even better, for him to walk away. Nothing anyone had taught me told me explicitly that this ritual was wrong but, in the solitude of his approach, I felt in every inch of my bones that it was. So ingrained were the rules of segregation between men and women that fathers didn't even touch their own daughters once they had turned twelve. It was implicit and unspoken that he was too close to me. I knew that this was his secret and my job was to protect it. I could only be this adult that he pretended I was if I was in his presence, and so I was trapped.

All of this led me to feeling that, again, I was alone and abandoned in circumstances that were out of my control. I couldn't keep up the tough-girl act when, in fact, I felt vulnerable and afraid. I wanted to check out of this ridiculous situation and this family that wasn't mine but I didn't have anywhere to go.

It was on a Sunday at the start of June that he suggested we take a trip to the Pennine Hills a couple of hours north of where we lived and take Rena with us, too, as a treat for her birthday. I was confused. I was the one he was meant to be treating like an adult. Why was he also giving my best friend this attention?

We all went: me, Rena, him, his wife and kids. It was early evening, but still hours from getting dark, when we parked up and walked from the car park to a clearing just over a ridge, where he set up a barbecue. I felt off-kilter, miserable. Todros unsettled me but he'd also hooked me on to the snippets of attention he offered up; now he was denying me even those, in favour of Rena and his family. The feeling of wanting an escape route descended again. I endured the meal but as we packed up and lumbered back to the car, I slipped off the path and headed off in another direction, unnoticed. Night was falling. I knew it was a stunt that would garner attention but that wasn't my motivation. I was just done. I wanted to get away from them.

I was wearing black flared jeans and a black polo shirt, neither modest nor climbing attire. On my feet were my favourite black leather lace-up shoes with platform soles. I scaled the rocky surface of the hill in them, crawling on my hands and knees until I came to a large, flat rock that served as a ledge, and sat down. It was almost dark and it had been at least two hours since I'd left the group, who would now have noticed I was missing. I was exposed to the elements with nothing at all to protect me or keep me from falling. I made my body small and huddled against the hillside. My phone rang. It was Search and Rescue.

'Your dad is really worried about you,' said the voice on the other end.

'He's not my father,' I shouted, hearing my voice echo through the valley.

I knew I was in danger but I was more preoccupied with holding on to the space I so wanted, in order to be alone. Being on that hillside was the safest and calmest I'd felt in a long time.

The voice told me a helicopter had been dispatched and asked me to wave my hands when it passed overhead. When it passed me, I shoved myself deep into a nearby crevice and waited for the sound of its rattling rotors to hover then fade away. I settled in for the night. I didn't want to be rescued.

I was shit-scared. I stayed there until first light, my phone ringing every so often as the guy from Search and Rescue called to check I was still alive. When morning came, I made my way down. When I reached the path – filthy, sweaty, tired and hungry – a police van was waiting at the end of it.

'Are you Yehudis Fletcher?' the officer asked.

'Yes.'

'Do you know how many people are looking for you?' he continued.

I looked at him with disdain. Then I looked past him at Todros, standing fifteen feet behind, with his arms held out to hug me. He hadn't done that before. In fact, no adult had held their arms out to hug me in a long time; I hadn't even spoken to my own parents since leaving Israel. Despite myself, I let him wrap his arms around me, pulling me into him. A forbidden embrace that lasted too long.

On the journey home, I slept in the passenger seat of his car. We didn't exchange a word but we arrived home to his wife's anger. She couldn't believe what I had done, how I had embarrassed their family. I was once again faced with a household of people who couldn't deal with me. Todros suggested that she and the children go to London to stay with his mother and recover from my cry for help, which they did that afternoon, leaving him and me in the house, alone. That night was the first time he sexually assaulted me.

I was lying in bed late at night, wearing a vest top and fake Adidas leggings with the wrong number of stripes down the side. I still had a girlish body and wore a maroon bra with a lace band underneath the two small cups. I wasn't used to anyone entering my room at night but Todros knocked on the door and walked in without waiting for a response. He was wearing a white vest and white cotton boxers. This horrified me. I shouldn't see him like that. I didn't want to. I had never seen any man in a state of undress. He sat on the end of my bed and pulled back the pink-striped duvet that had been covering me.

'Let me give you a massage,' he said.

In that tiny, enclosed space, with only us in the house, I didn't know how to say no.

'I can't do it properly with this on,' he growled, pulling at my flimsy top and waiting for me to take it off. I lay silent, frozen. I turned myself away from him, covering my chest with one hand and removing my vest with the other. I turned on to my tummy to cover my bee-sting breasts and felt his rough, calloused hands squeeze my shoulder blades. He moved them to the band of my bra, pulling it back, hard.

'I can't work with this on,' he said now.

I sat up quickly. He was frustrated and tugged it urgently, savagely. I have this excruciatingly slow memory of it moving through the air in front of me as he unhooked it and pulled it off. I was naked from the waist up.

He pushed me on to my back and lay on his side, between me and the wall. There wasn't space for both of us. The room was filled with silence but for his panting. He yanked down my leggings, pulling off my knickers at the same time. He was unhindered now. His hands reached between my legs and fiddled around.

'Where's your clit?' he commanded.

'Show me where your clit is.'

I'd read the word in magazines. I put my hand there. That was what he wanted to see. Me touching myself.

He shoved two fingers inside me.

I felt no pain because I wasn't in my body any more. My soul was suspended, watching the scene from above. He clambered on top of me and pressed his knees on either side of my chest, clamping them into my armpits. His penis was wide and erect, pushing through the window of his boxers, its tip touching my face. He tried to force it into my mouth. I clamped my jaw shut and moved my head from side to side: *No.* I should have bitten him.

I'd tied my hair back to sleep, in a long plait that was now trapped underneath me and the weight of him. The pain from the braid pulling as I tried to shake my head free was the only thing I could feel. He took my hands, which he had pinned above me, and wrapped them around his penis.

'Oh, make yourself useful,' he commanded, irritated by me.

I didn't know what I was supposed to do, so I lay there, static. He climbed off.

'I'm coming back in a minute,' he muttered as he hurried to the bathroom to finish himself off. I heard the toilet flush against the silence of the empty house and rushed to gather my clothes, pulling them on underneath my duvet. Then his face appeared at the open door.

'Goodnight,' he said. And left.

What now? The night threatened to last for ever as I lay there, shell-shocked, listening, dreading his return. At some point – I don't know how – I must have fallen asleep because, when I woke, my confusion had been supplanted by anger.

'Do you want a coffee?' he asked when I walked into the kitchen the next morning.

'No,' I said. 'I don't want coffee. I want to tell you that what happened last night can never happen again.'

'Don't worry,' he said breezily. 'That's not sex. I wouldn't have sex with you.'

'I know. You wouldn't want little blonde babies,' I said, cocky, naive, flustered, furious. 'Whatever you want to call last night, it can't happen again,' I repeated.

The sad part was I didn't know what last night had been at all. I didn't even register that I'd been violated. I just thought he'd done wrong in the context of his marriage. I had no idea that I was the victim of a crime, because no one had given me the words to know. Other than depictions in the movies I'd seen since coming back to Manchester, my understanding of sex hadn't developed any further than searching it up in encyclopaedias. There was a lot of discussion in magazines I read about who was having sex and when, but not what sex consisted of. I only knew it wasn't what I wanted.

The assaults continued almost nightly; at other times, too, if he ever caught me alone. I have no sense of how long each lasted but I began to write them down in a diary that I kept in my schoolbag. Maybe I had a feeling I would need to prove what had happened one day or maybe I just needed to make sense of it.

Sometimes, I tried to fight against him and he would beg. Sometimes, I didn't have the strength to fight. I came up with a hierarchy of what I would and wouldn't do to maintain some kind of semblance of control. I would allow him to push and rub himself on me or touch me, hoping he would not enter my mouth or vagina. It wasn't much, but it was the only thing that stopped me from losing it.

He'd drive me around in his car – either for the sake of it or after taking me to the dentist or the shops – and stop off at the office he sometimes used (although it was never clear what work he did there). He would try it while we were alone there, or, back at home, he'd pin me up against the door in his study, which was under my bedroom. He'd play CDs of classical music in the background that I'd try to use as a distraction tool, asking him to stop and listen to a track I claimed to like, to slow down what was happening to me. Frequently, I would walk out of the room to see his wife sitting on the bottom step in front of me, never a word or look exchanged between us. A small voice in my head wondered if she knew what was going on. She treated me as a rival, veering between being full of disdain and acting like a bossy mother.

When I showered at night, he'd pick the lock on the bathroom door to peer in at me. Once, he left a small teddy bear, with a loop on its head, hanging from the handle. When I returned to my bedroom, there was a text message from him: 'Did you get my calling card?'

He frequently attempted to kiss me on the lips and when I asked him to stop he'd say: 'Don't you want me to love you?'

'Yes,' I'd respond. 'But like a father.'

This went on for around six months. At school, I was doing well academically but they'd heard about my escape on the hillside and I was treated like a troublesome kid again. No one ever thought to ask what I was running from. I felt like I was living in parallel universes. My teachers viewed me as a naughty child but with Todros I was expected to be an adult.

I was exhausted all the time because, between the coffee he gave me each evening and the fear of him entering my room, I lay awake all night. In the daytime, my mind was preoccupied with what was happening to me at night. The fear of my secret spilling out made me withdraw into myself. I put a wedge between my friends and I talked to them less, I went out less and I enjoyed things less. The world had lost its sheen and my curiosity had gone. I stopped expecting anything – from myself, from my teachers, from my parents, and especially from G-d.

Todros eventually convinced me I was too mature for my classes altogether and my time should be spent learning Torah and how to be a proper Jewish young woman. I left school on his say-so and got a job in a print house earning £120 a week making wedding invitations for the families in my community. I took up lessons with Todros's aunt – the sort of lessons my mother used to offer young women – and I would use them to ask sexually explicit questions of her beyond those expected of a girl my age. She never asked why. I wished she would.

At the house, it became like a cat-and-mouse game. He would try to find me on my own, while I tried to regain power by evading and taunting him. I developed an edge. I started calling him by his first name, which embarrassed him. When he took me to the bank to open an account for himself, in my name, I sat on his lap – unheard of in public between a Charedi man and a young girl – as if to prove to him that if his love was that of a father, then this was just fine. I had nothing else at my disposal.

It was a night in October when it all changed. He was on my bed, on top of me, when his wife flung the door open.

'I knew it,' she yelled, her white cotton nightie billowing.

I'm fairly sure she saw what had happened as him cheating on her. He jumped off me and stared pleadingly at his wife. They left together and left me alone.

In the morning, he was waiting in the kitchen with coffee.

'You have to leave,' he said, barely looking at me.

I had nowhere to go.

'You made this mess, you sort it out,' I replied. 'I need somewhere to live.'

I left for work.

The next evening, he told me again: 'You have to go.'

He took matters into his own hands. Within forty-eight hours, he had found another rabbinical family nearby, also looking for lodgers. Another new place. Still alone. I packed my purple holdall, feeling powerless and terrified of what anyone might do to me next. Was this yet another case of jumping out of the frying pan and into the fire? Todros placed my bag in his car himself and drove me to the new family's door. I wouldn't be in a room with him again for ten years.

5

Are you a lesbian?

פָּנוּי הַבָּא עַל הַפְּנוּיָה שֶׁלֹּא לְשֵׁם אִישׁוּת עֲשָׂאָהּ זוֹנָה...אֲבָל אִשָּׁה פְּרִיצוּתָא בְּעָלְמָא

> ... an unmarried man who has intercourse with an unmarried woman not for the sake of marriage renders her a whore ... a woman's lewd behaviour with another woman is mere licentiousness.
>
> *Yevamos 76a*

MY NEW HOME WAS WARM and inviting. The rabbi and his wife included me in their household, where they had two sons living at home and an endless stream of married daughters who came and went with all their children. I joined in with family games the kids played, like who could stuff the most chocolate digestives in their mouth. Inside, however, I felt dead.

For months, I kept my torment to myself. I had nightmares when I slept, and looked around street corners when I went out, afraid he'd be there. I was a shell of a person, going through the motions needed to survive.

Encouraged by my maternal grandma, I spoke to my mother on the phone. There was no question of discussing what had happened with her – how could I, when we could barely talk about the weather without fighting – but Grandma suggested that I might ask to fly to Israel for a visit that November, to spend Chanukah with her, my father and Devorah. The idea initially seemed bonkers but there was a part of me that longed for any semblance of family, no matter how frayed our relationship was. I wanted to understand how much I had to hold on to. To my surprise, they agreed.

We spent the weekend as a family at a hotel resort in the north of the country, with my brothers and their families too. Devorah and I shared a room, enjoying the rare holiday atmosphere together. Devorah was thirteen now and her life had completely changed. She was living in a religious boarding school and spoke fluent Hebrew but still had her sweet, impish disposition. It was instantly clear to us both that we had missed one another terribly. We held on to every moment together, me braiding her hair and the two of us cuddling on the couch, sharing stories to catch up. But all the while I carried my secret with me and it created a single, unspoken chasm between us which we both skilfully ignored.

Chanukah is the Jewish 'festival of light', a time for celebration that, in Israel, is a national holiday period. It is marked by eight days of candle-lighting, and each night my family would gather with others in the hotel lobby to kindle the flames and sing songs. I would stay quiet while I watched enviously at other, non-Charedi women, who had the freedom to join in. When my father noticed me looking, I looked away.

Relations between my parents and me were just as tense as when I'd left. There was no depth to the conversations we shared, no talk of the last time I was in Israel and no querying how I felt now.

'Have you tried the new cheese in the buffet?' my mother would ask.

'No, but I must,' I would reply.

It was excruciating. I felt foolish for hoping things might be better. The only thing that was different was the absence of high drama. The stakes were lower now. I didn't have the energy to argue any more.

The night before I flew home, I visited the rabbi I'd called when I'd overdosed; he'd always spoken to me more frankly than other adults.

'Did he do something to you?' he asked me when I told him that I'd moved out of Todros's home.

I was shifty, so he asked outright: 'Did he sexually abuse you?'

I'd never heard that word: 'abuse'. I didn't know what it meant, but he didn't need to explain much for me to understand that this is how the rest of the world referred to what had happened to me.

'Yes,' I said quietly. 'He did.'

That night he didn't just teach me the word, he gave me something new: an expectation that something should be done about it.

When I flew home the next morning, I did so, uncomfortable in the discovery that there were words for what had happened to me. That it was a real thing and that Todros had known it was wrong, even when I hadn't. He was evil. It both shook my core and left me desperate to understand more. I called Rena from the departure lounge to tell her what he'd done. She said he'd once tried the same with her. The word was new to her as well and we sat at two ends of the same call, in stunned silence.

Back in Manchester, I found solace at my grandmother's house. Grandma G had been too frail to have me live with her but she knew how to be with me and we shared a closeness that was rare in my life. She was someone I could cry to. She lived in a mews house a short walk across the park from the house where I was lodging. She was in her eighties; a tall lady, shortened by the stoop of old age. Her pale-blue eyes were draped with crinkled lids and she was never without a kerchief or turban covering her pure-white hair, once the same auburn-brown as mine. I would walk over a couple of times a week to bathe her and wash her hair. Afterwards, she'd prepare a simple meal that we'd eat at the small dining table pushed up against the wall of her narrow kitchen, overlooking the street below.

During one such supper, a week after my return, I told her what had happened in Todros's home. Having been given the words, this was now something I could share, and I trusted Grandma's love more than anyone's. I knew I could confide in her. She put her face in her hands. When she looked up, there was blind, white fury in her eyes. She railed against him. She was angry for me and I took comfort in that. No one had ever been angry on my behalf before. For the first time in my life, I heard her swear. She called him a '*shtick dreck*' – 'piece of shit' in Yiddish.

Later, when we were calmer, she told me that she had been sexually abused too, when she was eleven. We shared our heavy stories, cried and even managed to laugh.

Now, the only two adults that I could rely on had given me the kind of validation that I needed and shown me I was a victim who had been wronged and was entitled to justice. No longer a secret, the abuse became something that I couldn't – wouldn't – shut up about.

I still didn't feel able to tell my parents; they had failed to keep me safe and I knew I couldn't rely on them to do that now, but I told my co-worker at the print house, a woman known in religious circles as an 'older single', which is to say she was unmarried at twenty-three. She told the print house manager, Declan – a brawny Salford native with big tattoos and a heart of gold – who came lumbering up the office's rickety stairs, overlooking the colossal print machinery, and asked my permission to tell our boss, the owner. The owner was a roly-poly Jewish man who, in turn, called his neighbour, a registrar of the Beth Din. The Beth Din is a court of Jewish law that presides over disputes and determines matters of right and wrong within a community that lives pragmatically and morally by religious, not state, statutes. That same week a call came through on the landline.

'Do you think you're his first?' the registrar on the other end opened with, offering more than just a suggestion that this wasn't the first complaint to be lodged either formally or informally against Todros. His voice sounded like gravel on the phone line, rebuking me, as though it had been remiss of me to even consider my abuse worth sharing. He asked me to write down my testimony and submit any supporting evidence. My tight scrawl covered four pages. I sent the teddy bear he'd hung on the bathroom door, and cut out and glued down pages of my diary, too. The upshot? In Jewish law, as a girl or woman, my word was worth less than the gluestick I'd used to assemble my evidence. Unless there had been a second man present to witness the abuse – which was clearly unlikely – according to community law it never happened. It wasn't that the court didn't believe me; I simply didn't matter. Telling the police was never even raised as a possibility. No one suggested it and I didn't even know the option existed. Matters of any and all gravitas were always dealt with inside the community.

The Beth Din summoned Todros and told him to go for therapy. A senior rabbi also suggested that his daughters wear dressing gowns when they left their bedrooms. I never got my evidence back.

I'd tried to get justice and I'd been silenced. I still hadn't heard from my parents – in fact I had no idea if they knew what had gone on or not – and I was in charge of fixing the damage that Todros had done to me, and now my reputation for complaining, for myself. I had to get out of Manchester and back on track.

I had just turned sixteen. I had all the hardship of adulthood but none of the legitimacy that came with it. The only way to achieve acceptable status within my community, indeed any legitimacy at all, was to get married; it was the only way I would be allowed it. My sisters had both married at eighteen and my brothers' brides had been around that age, too. That was only two years away. Most of the neighbourhood knew what had happened to me and, now that I was viewed as damaged goods, I was acutely aware that I was at the bottom of the 'prospective wife' pile. Regardless, finding a husband was the only way to continue living within a community as anything other than a teenage girl who'd been abused. If I was ever going to shake off the shadow of Todros, moving away and making myself marriageable was my only option.

So, I did what other religious girls my age were doing. I went to Israel to learn how to be a wife. I applied to a 'sem' – a religious seminary, which would teach me how to think, study scriptures and transition into adulthood the 'right' way. With me seemingly back on a more suitable path, my parents were happy to pay for this education, so I set about finding one I liked the look of. Sem was essentially wife school, and there were tiers: top ones suited to good girls who were 'well placed' to absorb the knowledge already, and a second kind of institution aimed at girls like me, who needed a more targeted approach including extra trips to the beach and a marginally more lax dress code to keep them engaged. The prestigious ones didn't want me – I knew I could be diligent but my frequent moves and stop-start schooling, coupled with my family's social status, which wasn't rabbinical top-drawer, hinted at neither a pious nor desirable student – but I was accepted into a smaller sem called Keshet. Its name, meaning rainbow, was soon changed to distance itself from appearing pro-gay rights.

The seminary was spread over a couple of apartments just up the hill from my parents' flat in Beit Shemesh. I would live and learn with four other girls and, on our first day, I introduced myself to them like this: 'My name is Yehudis, I come from England, my parents live here and I'm a survivor of sexual abuse.'

I accompanied my intro with an outstretched arm, poised to shake a hand. Even without the jaw-dropping opener, this gesture was extremely forthright for any sixteen-year-old, let alone a new student at a seminary for religious girls. What happened to me was so persistently present in my mind that owning it became part of the shield I developed to survive.

Naturally, my introduction provoked discomfort in others, but the secondary effect of my brazen honesty was miraculous. One by one, the girls told me their secrets. One confided she had been raped in the street by two men and we'd frequently cry together. The girls offloaded so much of their own trauma that before long we were close friends.

The sem education failed to stimulate me almost entirely. I was interested in exploring ideas, not receiving them, and so I got very little out of it. One of the rabbis looked exactly like Todros, so I refused to go to his class. In other lessons, I read Sidney Sheldon books that I bought at the second-hand bookshop in the centre of town. They were completely inappropriate and hiding them behind my religious texts could get me thrown out – not that I was invested enough in the calibre of the education to consider that a threat.

A typical week consisted of Bible study, learning the laws of how to keep a kosher kitchen and classes in Jewish thought. This meant deepening our understanding of what was and wasn't an appropriate way to think, as future wives. These classes were always delivered by men, who taught us that male and female domestic roles were prescribed as separate but equal and there was no room to question that paradigm. As wives we should not turn our minds to our own egos. We were allowed to empower our husbands to make the right choices; we simply couldn't make those decisions ourselves.

We learned which part of our leg could be exposed (from the knee down, according to some opinions, although not my father's) and what we were and were not allowed to read in the Torah: we could continue to learn the stories but not the law. There was one rabbi, who taught us the laws of divorce – which in itself was unexpected – who cheated by photocopying pages so that we were reading off a sheet fresh from the printer and not technically the original text, a practice that was forbidden to women. This thrilled us all. Even within this stringent setting among the men in black coats, there were rule-benders and G-d still seemed to accept them. I had felt distant from G-d since the abuse but now, privately, I began to reconsider whether there was indeed valuable mileage in my less conservative approach to G-d and His rules, too. There must be space for me. Maybe it didn't have to be all or nothing?

As I was back in Israel, I sometimes visited my parents at the weekends and argued with my father about these deviations in religious thinking. Inevitably, I would hear from a teacher, on Monday, making clear that their opinions were in the minority and that I shouldn't follow them, having received a complaint from my father. Daddy couldn't retract the thought that had lodged itself in my brain, though.

In the meantime, I made the most of partying with my friends, which is far less surprising than you'd expect for religious kids who aren't meant to listen to secular music or mix with the opposite sex. There were thousands of teenagers who'd come to Jerusalem to study as I had, and we found ways of adhering to the rules without entirely adhering to them. There was expected separation in public spaces, which the adults tried their best to enforce, but there was, of course, a subculture of horny young people who 'hung out' in closer and closer proximity to one another as the hours went on, eventually mixing, talking, flirting and even coupling off, knowing full well that to do so was utterly scandalous. For a large group of such particularly religious teenagers, who observed *shabbos* and modesty rules, and who lived otherwise strictly observant lives, this indulgence in exploring a place where the rules were stretched and even broken was something of a commonplace coming-of-age. Our capacity to explore our emerging adult selves may have been much narrower than that of other teens but the desire to find a little space to have fun and experiment with our world was the same.

Every Thursday night before the weekend, which begins on Friday in Israel, my friends and I would take two busses from Beit Shemesh to the centre of Jerusalem and crowd into the tiny bars built into its stone streets in our long denim skirts and oversized hoodies. My parents didn't give me any spending money so I frantically babysat to buy my friends and myself blue shots called Polish Butterflies that cost five shekels (about ninety pence sterling) and got us drunk the fastest. Orthodox men got drunk plenty – in fact whisky and wine were a big cultural feature of *shabbos* and festivals. Women weren't meant to, lest they take their clothes off or speak up, but we did it anyway.

The apartment we lived in was disgusting because it was left to us teenagers to clean it ourselves. At one point we found a puppy in the playground down the road and brought it home to live with us, making its bed in one of the two showers. We kept vodka in the freezer that I often drank for breakfast. Weed was a treat that we sometimes got hold of from older boys who went to male-equivalent institutions a couple of streets away. None of what we were doing was forbidden, exactly. There is no rule to say you can't smoke and drink. It was just considered unseemly, and, if anyone found out, it would impact our marriage prospects. It was the freest I'd ever felt.

I visited my parents fairly regularly. They were content, relieved even, that I was focusing my sights on marriage, but we still argued constantly about everything I did or didn't do. I recall one particular row where my mother went on and on about Manchester and Todros, and how I'd clearly messed up something else. I exploded at her.

'Todros abused me!'

'Shh,' she hushed, eyes darting back and forth, hoping the neighbours couldn't hear, then: 'Why didn't you lock the door?'

I was rendered speechless. The bar was on the floor and she couldn't even meet it. I had felt failed by her before but now, with every inch of my being, I believed she was a terrible mother.

There was another new dimension to life in the sem apartment. For the first time, I was living in an all-girls environment. This meant that, within those four walls, modesty laws needn't be enforced. In other words, clothes were optional. We'd borrow outfits from each other and get undressed in front of one another or nip down to the shared shower in nothing but a towel. It never once crossed my mind that I could have sex with these girls. That kind of love was not part of my lexicon; I had no idea it was possible. However, I admired their bodies, and my own, and loved these moments of shared intimacy in our day-to-day lives.

One day, during a walk down the dry and dusty hillside to synagogue, a fellow student, an American girl called Tova, who was part of our friendship group, turned to me and said: 'Can I ask you something?'

The two of us fell behind. 'There's nothing wrong . . .' she started. 'But are you a lesbian?'

'Why would you say that?' I wondered out loud. I'd never so much as heard the word, let alone known what it meant. I would later learn that, in Jewish law, sex between women is invisible. In the book of Leviticus, the Torah wedges homosexuality within a list of prohibitions, including child sacrifice and bestiality, but lesbians don't have the honour of being acknowledged, never mind forbidden. Instead, the law only teaches that such relations between women are 'mere licentiousness' and they should be returned to their husbands should a dalliance ensue. In biblical times, this was not real enough a betrayal of marriage as to be punishable by death, which was the recommended punishment for a man found lying with a man. Lesbians didn't matter enough to be given the death penalty, but that still didn't mean there was space for them. Women loving and satisfying each other was the antithesis of the strict, gendered expectations that were in place and, most threatening of all, acknowledged that women have sexual desire all of their own.

Tova extrapolated: 'You're always trying to get people to notice your body,' she said hesitantly. 'It's like you want us to look at you.' As her questions continued, her words helped me to crystallize the concept she was explaining. I realized, much like the first time I heard the word abuse, that it described me with clarity. Once again, I had been offered a window into an experience that I never knew existed. It felt like another facet of myself had been unlocked. I was desperate to know more.

A few days later, I was chopping vegetables at my mother's kitchen table while she stood over the sink, washing dishes with her back to me. I had no idea of the enormity of what I'd discovered; I certainly hadn't read between the lines of Leviticus yet. Maybe if I told Mummy she would help me to understand more? I could offer it up like an olive branch, another chance for her to be my confidant, after shutting down the abuse.

I let the words come out: 'Do you know, Mummy, I think I'm a lesbian.'

'No you're not,' she replied without glancing up from her crockery. She didn't take the branch.

Dissatisfied, I went to see my rabbi friend and at the end of our visit, as he saw me out of the gate to his building, I mustered up the courage to try again. 'I think I'm a lesbian.'

'Of course you are,' he said matter-of-factly. 'All the girls in my sem are sleeping with each other. It's normal. It goes away when you get married.'

Now I *had* to find a husband.

6

Woman of valour

אֵשֶׁת־חַיִל מִי יִמְצָא וְרָחֹק מִפְּנִינִים מִכְרָהּ

What a rare find is a woman of valour. Her worth is far beyond that of rubies.

Proverbs 31:10

In charedi circles, there is no other way to graduate into adulthood than through heterosexual marriage. The praying, the learning, the blessing of food and thanking G-d, the covering up and washing hands, it was all geared towards being a good wife. From the moment I was born, I was a wife and mother in training. As an abuse victim and a lesbian, neither of which my community would be able to accept, I had all the more reason to get hitched. As a married woman, the difficult aspects of my personality would apparently conveniently disappear and I could move on with my life as a respected adult.

During one of my Jerusalem nights out, I exchanged numbers with an English guy, Chezki, a Chasidic teen two years older, with curled *peyos* in front of his ears. While groups of boys socialized in the vicinity of girls in group situations, in central Jerusalem, an unmarried male and female were not permitted to spend time together in private. This meant that if a teenage couple were getting to know one another, which could only ever happen with a view to marriage following an approved introduction by their parents, they must meet in public: a hotel lobby, a park or a cafe, say. As I'd learned during my time in Israel, however, this didn't mean that you couldn't bend the rules. Young couples would often find private spots in supposedly public spaces. So, Chezki and I, although our introduction had not been formally arranged, met in a graveyard, at night, where he used an early opportunity – again, informally – to get his penis out.

Confronted by his thing I said, 'I'm sorry, I can't do this,' and left abruptly.

When I got home he texted, asking what was going on. I told him it didn't feel right, so he offered to take me to a hotel instead.

'I don't want to give you my virginity,' I tapped into my phone.

'Don't worry,' he typed back. 'We can do it up your arse.'

We didn't. But he did become my boyfriend. It wasn't that he offered me anything that might have seemed like a first taste of romance, but he gave me the time of day and he didn't abuse me. Compared to my other experiences with men, this made him seem like an acceptable suitor. Given we were dating, we believed we were on the path to marriage. We began seeing each other regularly, which occasionally extended to a hand job at a graveside.

I don't know how much my parents did or didn't know about what I was doing, but it was clear that I wasn't conforming: I'd been kicked out of sem by now (after the Sidney Sheldon books were discovered) and was living with them again, temporarily. I didn't look the part of a modest premarriageable girl waiting to be matched and I didn't play the part either. Before I could deliver any more scandal upon my family, they decided some time back in England, again, would do me good, and this time they sent me to live with my brother Dov Ber, who was married with three kids. Leaving my only friends felt like a loss but, as far as Chezki was concerned, international matches were perfectly usual so I presumed I'd just see him again when we got married. In my mind I was still firmly on the path to wifehood and, with that, adulthood.

I hadn't seen or spoken to Dov Ber for months. He was my favourite older brother but, regardless, we didn't have much of a connection. He lived in Gateshead – a town where 6,000 Charedi Jews inhabit six densely populated streets. His house was on a steep hill that was so thick with snow when I arrived in February 2005 that the taxi bringing me from the train station had no chance of climbing it. The driver dropped me at the bottom, leaving me to wheel my purple holdall up the slope, through the icy sludge, to his front door.

Dov Ber was preparing to open a kosher burger takeaway and the family hoped I'd be put to good use serving the community of Gateshead. The Jewish corner of town was like a university neighbourhood except there is only one degree available: Torah. The inhabitants were so *frum* that there were different grocery-shop time slots for unmarried males and for females, lest their paths cross.

Another new place. I didn't dare feel optimistic enough to call it 'home'. There was nothing for it but to reinvent myself again. I was six months off eighteen. I still spoke to Chezki daily on the phone but the message from those around me was that I needed to become someone that people other than him deemed suitable for marriage. By simple virtue of us meeting on our own, without first being set up by our guardians, we could never have been a good enough match for my family. I put away the trendy clothes I loved and bought a cheap, conservative wardrobe of black tights and ballet pumps, cardigans, blouses and A-line skirts. Privately, of course, I was unchanged and spent nights behind my bedroom door reading and rereading the dog-eared pages of *DIVA* magazine that my friend Penina, who I'd met at summer camp, sent up from London every month, wrapped in discreet brown paper.

Publicly, I got on with the business of appearing acceptable with wifely potential. I didn't really give a shit who my husband was going to be – Chezki or any man would do. I just needed the autonomy that married life promised. A couple of months later, Chezki was visiting family in London, so we met up. He thought I looked hotter than ever in my new chaste clothing and we decided to try again with our quest to marry.

I hated living in other people's houses and I really just wanted the whole thing done with. If I could get married, I'd have my own home, my own space. Leah, my most devout older sister, was living in London's Stamford Hill with a family of her own and took on a motherly role for me, too. She knew nothing of my and Chezki's relationship, so we tried to engineer a *shidduch* (a match) in which she would agree to us 'meeting' – but, somehow, word of our existing romance reached her. There are rules for the start of a respectable marriage: an adult has to suggest the *shidduch* and any further meetings, then the proposal, are agreed upon by the parents. The couple in question are not to have any hand in it, so when Leah found out the truth, she was furious. Chezki returned to Israel and our engagement was never approved.

Back in Gateshead, Dov Ber's burger takeaway had failed to take off. He had bought the premises and all of the equipment but had been refused the kosher accreditation needed to serve his religious public, since the men with beards were afraid that boys and girls might too easily mix there. I was expected to contribute to the household and certainly cover my own costs, so I was now holding down three jobs to support myself. Mornings were spent in a travel agency that served the community's need to fly to weddings and births, followed by afternoon shifts in Mr Dansky's kosher grocery store. Mr Dansky was a cantankerous man who made filthy, deadpan jokes, but he cared about me and would offer me sandwiches while ordering the boys who worked there to shlep stock so I didn't have to. I loved my position of authority there, policing queues and having a little piece of power for once.

My final work shift of the day was doing accounts for Mr Honig, an externally devout looking businessman from one of Gateshead's most respected families, who ran his office from a terrace house. The fact that I was virtually innumerate didn't seem to matter to Mr Honig, but placing our desks next to one another and finding fifty reasons a day to lean over and glance at the outline of my boobs did.

A few nights a week, I attended evening school in a small learning centre attached to the house of a lady called Mrs Halpern, a gentle woman with a soft face and green eyes, in an attempt to gain some GCSEs. We completed random papers that were occasionally sent off for marking. I never received the results of a single one but, after lessons, Mrs Halpern would invite me through a door marked PRIVATE into the tiny kitchen of the home she shared with her husband and eleven children. She and I would sit at her table and read deep, philosophical Jewish texts together, which was very unusual but fortunately no one pulled us up on it. It was the kind of conversation I relished and rarely got elsewhere.

That August, I turned eighteen. In October, during a visit to Miriam's, she told me a *shidduch* had come up. A man who'd made a name helping at-risk teens in her family's community to get back on their feet knew a young man he thought I should meet. Danny was five years older than me and had also been through a lot, but wanted to settle down.

'He will kiss the floor you walk on,' the man boasted. That sounded fine to me.

While my parents, who were in only occasional contact, viewed marrying me off as the only acceptable way to sort me out, they weren't terribly invested in the process itself; not in the same way they had been for my sisters. They'd already written off any belief that I could be a good little wife and certainly weren't going to expend any energy on helping me. But I heard through the Jewish grapevine, which is nothing if not swift and reliable, that my boss at the Gateshead travel agency knew of Danny. I asked for her opinion of him. Her first response was concern: 'He's not the most straightforward,' she offered cryptically. It sounded ominous and I trusted her so I considered this, briefly. But the louder message from everyone else, implicitly and sometimes explicitly, was: 'You know who you are; you may not get a better offer.'

My parents agreed, from Israel, and a meeting was set up in Leah's dining room. Leah's house was a two-up, two-down not far from Miriam's. The dining room was tiny, formalized by a china cabinet and mahogany table. The table was bare – no food should be eaten before any '*mazel tov*' was proclaimed – and Leah and her husband sat on either side of me, Danny and his parents across from us.

Danny was handsome in a little-boy way. He trimmed his beard short and neat – a sign of his rebellion, because the Bible says, 'You shall not round off the corners on your head, or destroy the corners of your beard.' He wore a fresh haircut, an immaculately cut suit and Gucci loafers. His parents had also brought a woman with them, Mrs Blau, who was their age and introduced as his mentor who had moved here from a community in New York, where she had been a prominent figure. She was more intriguing to me than Danny's mother, who was plainly dressed and quiet. Mrs Blau was, by contrast, expensively dressed in a fine-knit pastel twinset, mid-length straight skirt and Ferragamo pumps. She wore her stiff, chin-length, chestnut-brown wig under a pillbox hat and spoke in a booming American accent.

My brother-in-law and Danny's father made introductions

for us all and, following fifteen minutes' small talk, Danny and I were left alone, the door slightly ajar to keep us in public view. We mustered up half an hour's awkward conversation, each of us studiously ignoring what we had already been told about each other, which was that we matched because we were both damaged. When Danny's father knocked on the door to indicate that our time was up, we were both relieved to be able to drop the act.

This whole process followed a tried-and-tested formula where the aim was to reach the endgame as quickly as possible. Our families must have discussed their approval while we were speaking that day because a phone call came from Mrs Blau the next morning relaying that Danny would pick me up for another date the following afternoon. This speed of matchmaking was absolutely typical: the transaction had already been arranged; now they just had to make sure we could bear each other's company.

'You are checking to see he has a nose in the middle of his face, nothing more,' Leah had advised.

Danny pulled up at Leah's in his blue BMW and drove me to a central London hotel, speeding most of the way and stopping on a double yellow line outside the entrance.

'Are you sure you can park here?' I asked.

'You can park anywhere,' he replied. 'It just costs £80.'

He bowled up to the hotel door and was promptly refused entry for not wearing a tie, so, as quickly as he'd dumped the car, he drove me back home in it.

'There's something you need to know,' I said as he raced through the streets of north-east London. I was less bothered about the date being cut short than my opportunity to disclose what had happened to me. It was something I'd been wrangling with since our introduction. Telling him felt like an obstacle I had to clear before we could get engaged.

'Don't worry,' he said. 'They've already told me. It's fine.' That felt easy.

He picked me up again on Saturday night, sporting what I now identified as a third pair of Gucci shoes. I was under no illusion that four days and not quite three dates after we had met, he was going to propose. It was how things were done, and anyway, I caught Leah laying the table with celebratory cakes as I left the house.

I didn't feel the excitement that I'd heard some new brides talk about; it was more a buzz of confidence that things were back on track. I was on my way to a respectable adulthood. I had put on a black pencil skirt with a black pinstripe shirt tucked in, that I thought looked sexy, in a powerful way.

'When we get married, you're not going to wear clothes like that,' Danny declared.

He said he wanted to buy me expensive clothes, instead. I had never had luxury and something about his demeanour made me scared to say 'no'.

We drove through the Blackwall Tunnel towards Greenwich. The conversation wasn't stilted this time; there was banter between us and he made me laugh.

'You've got a spot on your forehead,' Danny pointed out.

I felt mortified. I flipped down the mirror to look. Written in red lipstick were the words: 'Will you marry me?'

I don't even think I said 'yes'. That had already been decided by someone else: I would be his bride, his *eshes chayil* – a woman of valour whose life's work was to sustain him. There were no tears of joy, no squeals of excitement or promises of endless devotion. I was just relieved this part was over.

Our wedding was set for twelve weeks later, 8 January 2006.

A month beforehand, Danny and I both began weekly lessons on how to be a husband and wife, respectively – Danny with the rabbi and me with the rebetzen, the rabbi's wife. The lessons were like the ones my mother used to deliver in Glasgow. Now that I was the bride, maybe I would get some of the answers that I'd been listening for when I pressed my ear against Mummy's door as a child. I arrived at a tall, modern front door that was opened by a petite woman with a bobbed, brown wig who invited me into her dining room. I was clearly nervous and she tried to set me at ease, offering me a seat at the table. Her tone was conspiratorial and I recognized the same books that my mother had, laid out between us.

The first lessons established the rules around purity, which, determined by my cycle, would be among the most sacred I would ever follow. These all-important guidelines would provide us with the twelve to fourteen days a month when we should avoid sex, touching and even sleeping in a bed together, for whoever touches a woman during her menstruation becomes impure themselves. For this reason, most Charedi homes have beds that can be pulled apart or pushed together according to when a wife is pure enough for her husband to touch. The rebetzen taught me that I was to wear black knickers at all times except for the seven days after my period, when I should wear white, allowing me to notice any further impure blood. I wrote everything down in a notebook, relishing this glimpse into adult life.

For the fourth and final lesson, she took me into the living room and sat me down on a sofa. I knew what was coming.

'I know that you know some things but I don't know what you know,' she began, uncomfortably skirting around the fact I'd been abused.

She then drew line drawings of male and female anatomies, on two separate pieces of card, and used her pen to point to the penis.

'This goes into there,' she said, tapping her pen on the vagina.

This was the first explanation I'd been given of what was expected on my wedding night. Even when I'd looked up sex in the dictionary as a child, I'd never quite understood the mechanics of it all. Magazines offered no real clarity. I'd avoided Chezki's attempts to show me how it worked. Would it really fit? I was sure it would hurt. Finally, here was my opportunity to ask questions. Her other brides might have been shocked but I was pragmatic.

Teachings dictate that, in the week before they wed, neither the bride nor groom must be left alone, lest they be snatched by a demon. So, they are allocated a *shomer* (chaperone) to watch over them. I chose Grandma G, who spent seven days and nights with me at Leah's. I also took a progesterone pill to ensure that my wedding fell exactly one week after my period, guaranteeing purity – which is to say the absence of any menstrual blood – for my new husband on our wedding night. This practice is so common that they are known as *kallah* (bridal) pills, rather than contraception, which they can only be used for if approved by a rabbi.

In preparation for the wedding night, for the week before my wedding I had to carry out twice-daily inspections of myself, wrapping a small, white cloth around my middle finger, inserting it into my vagina then holding it up to the light to check for staining. The pill ensured that this went to plan and, after seven clean days, it fell to Miriam to walk me to the *mikveh* – a ritual bath in which I was to immerse myself for my final preparations for marriage and purity.

The *mikveh* was in a purpose-built annex to the synagogue near Miriam's home, with its own entrance away from that of the main synagogue, to allow for discretion. Married women attended once a month at the end of their periods and were required to go at night, unseen. Brides-to-be, however, were permitted in daytime. Before we entered, Miriam beckoned me to one side and presented me with a gift: a lilac washbag with 'Yehudis' embroidered on it in white cotton. It contained nail scissors, an emery board and ear buds – everything you need to inspect and clean your body before entering the water each month. There was also a small laminated card reminding me of the steps I should take to cleanse thoroughly and in accordance with Torah law: cut your finger- and toenails; clean the corners of your ears, inside your ears, the crevices of your nipples and the depths of your belly button; wash your hair; use the toilet.

I thanked her; this gift was meant to make me feel like a proper woman, but it only drew attention to the apprehension that was beginning to swirl inside me at the thought of being seen naked by the old woman who tended to the *mikveh*. I reached for the doorbell. The attendant, a squat woman in her sixties, with a wig and printed housecoat, welcomed us inside and wished Miriam, not me, *mazel tov*.

She showed me to a small bathroom where I was to cleanse myself in a first bath before entering the ritualistic *mikveh* water, while Miriam sat down on a folding chair in the hallway, praying for my marriage and fertility. I did as the attendant instructed: drew myself a bath to clean myself, undressed then lowered myself into its hot water, hugging my knees to my little breasts. The servitude of this experience is intended to feel holy but I felt scared and vulnerable, as though I was fulfilling a duty I had no say in, welding the next link in a chain made by generations of women who had gone before me.

'Women in the Soviet Union would immerse in freezing lakes, cutting a hole in the ice during the winter,' my mother, who was in town for the wedding, had said to me before I left for the *mikveh*.

I let the water run; I couldn't remember the last time I'd filled a bath as deep as I wanted. I went through the laminated reminders in my head, stepped out, then looked at my body in the mirror and – as I had been instructed by the rebetzen who had been my bridal teacher – counted each of my body's orifices, touched them and said aloud, to myself and to G-d: 'I've checked it.'

I drained the bath then climbed back into the tub, turned on the taps and shivered while I waited for the shower above to splutter to life. I rinsed my body once more and combed carefully through my hair to ensure there were no knots. My skin felt hot to the touch but I was shaking. Alone and exposed, I felt the gravity of my impending marriage. I wrapped myself in the cardboard-stiff terry robe hanging on the back of the door and pushed my feet into a pair of yellow

Crocs that had been left out for me, then rang the bell to signal I was ready for the next part. The attendant arrived on the other side of the door and called for me to come through.

The *mikveh* itself was smaller than I had imagined: a 4ft by 5ft arctic-blue tiled pool, filled with warm water not quite clear enough to see to the bottom. The attendant asked me to hold out my hands and checked every nail and nail bed for snags that might harbour dirt. She used her right foot to drag a plastic stool in front of me and motioned for me to put my feet on it, one at a time, so she could inspect each toenail and then the soles. Finally, she ran her hands through my hair, checking for loose strands that might come away and contaminate my immersion.

Following her cues, I loosened my arms in the robe's sleeves and she lifted it off my body. I was naked in front of her. Until now, the water had felt intimidating. Suddenly, it was something that could shield me from this stranger's gaze. I felt my way down its five steps and let the water swallow me while she watched. Before I reached the final one, I passed her my glasses, which meant I could no longer see, but there was now nothing between the water – between purity – and me. I recalled what I'd been taught: immerse your whole head and body, bent over like a woman kneading bread. I felt the water flow into my most private spaces – that was the point of standing that way. I held my breath as long as I could and remembered I was meant to be praying for my marriage and fertility, but I was anxious to move on to the next step. Coming up for air, the acoustics elevated the attendant's voice as she cried '*Kosher!*' The rules required two more submersions and two more cries, after which I made my way back up the steps. I shivered with cold and embarrassment as I reached for my glasses.

'*Mazel tov*,' she said and led me back to the bathroom, where I climbed into my clothes, my skin still wet.

Miriam was waiting, her face damp with tears from her impassioned prayers for my marriage. She kissed me but I felt wooden. The ritual hadn't elevated or enlightened me; it had allowed my fear about what came next, and who I was expected to become, to seep deeper into my bones. I'd made the practical transition into womanhood that was required of me, but why did I have to do it naked in front of a sixty-year-old woman? Adulthood, marriage and sex all seemed terrifying and real now.

Back at Leah's, I packed some final items into a bag and went to a flat down the road belonging to Mrs Blau's friend, where I would spend the final twenty-four hours before my marriage contemplating and praying with Grandma G. We had supper together, I painted my nails a milky pale pink and we went to bed in the master bedroom, in two single beds made up in heavy sunflower-patterned damask bedding. We talked until the early hours with the lamps on – I can't remember about what – and slept for the final few hours until daylight.

Later that morning, I opened the door to a man in his forties with a collar-length grey beard and curled *peyos*, who introduced himself as a videographer. I had no idea who he was but he'd been sent by Mrs Blau to film me getting ready. He set up lights as more people I hadn't expected arrived to do my make-up and hair. Mrs Blau arrived too. She seemed to know who everyone was, even if I didn't. I sat on a dining chair in the middle of the living room, being primped while Grandma tsk-tsked at the amount of foundation they were trowelling on. When I looked in the mirror, I saw a different girl looking back: my hair was pushed back and curled softly around my shoulders, with a Swarovski crystal tiara set on top. My make-up was simple, in nude tones. The only tiny hint towards my personality was the turquoise eyeliner that I insisted the make-up artist use. Grandma came with me to the bedroom to help me into my dress: I was a tiny size six in a full-skirted, off-white silk creation with a high neck, long, puffy sleeves and intricate floral embroidery around my waist. She zipped up the back and I suddenly remembered how hungry I was; a bride must fast on her wedding day – it is her personal Yom Kippur, her holy day of atonement before entering marriage.

In the living room my stomach growled as the hair stylist pinned a long net veil to the back of my head and Grandma fastened my wedding jewellery: a white-gold watch with a diamond-encrusted rim around the face and a diamond necklace, both gifts from Danny. The necklace was heavy and scratchy. I knew he was giving me matching earrings after the wedding ceremony to wear at our party, but for now I wore my favourite silver dangly pair.

Women started arriving to have photos taken with me: my mother, mother-in-law, endless aunts and cousins. I felt like a chess piece being pushed around a board. The real me was completely lost under layers of make-up and frills. At 2 p.m., I paused to offer my afternoon prayer, alone in the kitchen. I repented and asked forgiveness: for being so tempting that Todros had sinned on my account, for being a lesbian, for

Chezki, for not having come to this day the way I should have done – pure. I wanted to emerge from the wedding canopy – the *chuppah* – that evening untarnished, ready, normal. It was a relief to get away from the women in the other room, taking pictures and chatting feverishly. I finished my prayers a little too quickly so I lingered for as long as possible until someone came looking for me.

A white vintage car that might have been a Rolls-Royce – I didn't care enough to notice – drove me the short distance to my ceremony venue: a school hall. This was an entirely normal choice for a religious wedding that could easily exceed five hundred guests, and where practicality and proximity to the community therefore dictated location.

On one side of the hall, a line of trestle tables was set with an enormous buffet of finger sandwiches, cream cakes and fruit carved into flowers and little swans. My nieces and nephews were running around getting chocolate down their wedding clothes and I was taken to sit on a throne-like wicker chair with a clam-shell back decorated with white fabric and ribbon. I was the centre of attention in a way that I'd never experienced before and I felt like an interloper.

I couldn't stop thinking about the sensation of my wedding dress weighing down my body, knowing that the next time I took it off, I'd be undressed in front of my husband.

My mother and mother-in-law stood on either side of me in a room full of around two hundred women. Classical music played in the background and women queued for me to bless them, each holding the belief that I'd repented so hard that I was now without sin. The music slowed to a march as the voices of men fervently singing approached from down the hall. My groom was led towards me by his father and mine, the arms of all three linked, dozens more males following behind in song. Their voices climbed to a crescendo. I smiled up at Danny and saw he was crying loudly. This was the *bedeken*, a pre-ceremony where he was expected to check my face to ensure that I was his intended – a tradition that had endured since biblical times, when Jacob was tricked into marrying Leah instead of her younger sister, his true love, Rachel.

Danny's eyes didn't meet mine but he looked dutifully over my face before he was guided away, the men still singing and he still crying. My mother pinned a second veil of opaque white satin to my hair, to hang over my face. By design, I couldn't see through it – and the men watching the ceremony wouldn't be exposed to my face. I was now walked to the *chuppah*, four poles with a navy-blue, gold-embroidered velvet cover balanced across the top, set up in the school playground, facing east to Jerusalem.

It was dusk. There were four hundred people crammed into the playground, men on one side, women on the other. I'd never been more visible, yet I didn't know who I was. My mother lifted my veil briefly, only twice, during the twenty-minute ceremony, once for me to take a sip of the wine that sanctified our marriage and again as Danny smashed a glass beneath his right foot at the end – a pause to grieve the destruction of the Temple in Jerusalem – before returning to a moment of joy.

Danny took me by the hand – it felt secure, strong – as we walked through crowds of well-wishers towards a small wooden door with two bearded men on either side. These were our witnesses and their job was to ensure we passed a few minutes alone in this room – the *yichud* (seclusion) room – together as husband and wife. My bridal teacher had told me that Danny would kiss me in there. I was anxious to get it over and done with and I waited, wondering each time he moved if this would be it. But he didn't kiss me. Instead of married, I felt rejected and confused. We broke our fast and all I could think was that my breath must smell and the smoked salmon sandwiches that had been left for us would make it worse. We felt awkward in this sudden, forced intimacy and said little, smiling stiltedly and eating to wait out the ten minutes or so before the men knocked and said '*Mazel tov*'. We were now officially married.

Before we left for our party venue, a woman bustled into the small room, holding a hatbox with the *sheitel* (wig) I had chosen for married life. She set herself up, clearing away sandwiches and laying out hairstyling equipment before pulling out the wig. For men, covering their head with a *cappel* is a reminder that G-d is above them; for women the teaching is that once she is no longer a virgin, her sexual energy beams from the top of her head and must be contained. The wig in front of me looked like a small part of me – long, soft, brown locks – spread out across the table. She arranged it on my head, pulling my own hair into a knot and tucking it away underneath. It was meant to stay covered for ever.

The maybe-Rolls-Royce drove us to The Decorium, a neoclassical banqueting venue near Alexandra Palace. Danny's parents had chosen it and it was opulent and ostentatious, with chandeliers dangling everywhere. As soon as I stepped inside the building I was beckoned for family photos, but first, I wanted a peek at the banqueting hall itself before everyone else arrived. I pulled at one of the double doors and poked my head through the gap. I was confronted with thousands and thousands of sunflowers. In January. Every table centrepiece and an entire wall was bright yellow, in bloom. Down the middle of the room was a *mechitza* – a divide so female and male guests could eat and dance out of sight of one another – that was decorated with sunflowers, too. My new father-in-law appeared behind me.

'Do you like them?' he beamed. 'I remember you said you love sunflowers. I spent ten grand on them.'

I couldn't make sense of the scale of his gesture but I smiled back politely and closed the door.

Fuck, I thought to myself. *Who* are *these people?*

In front of the camera, Danny held my hand and put his arm on my waist. We both knew how to put on public displays. While our guests sat down to their first course, chicken soup, we were served ours in a private room and he presented me with the diamond earrings to match the necklace that had since set off an allergic reaction. It was as much time as we'd spend together all night, as we were then shown to our respective top tables – one for men, one for women, both set against the wall of sunflowers. I walked into a whirlpool of dance, circles of women twirling to the Chasidic music that was being thumped out by a big band set up on Danny's side. With no men in view, this was our opportunity to have fun and each guest wanted her turn dancing with the bride. I loved it. I'd never felt so popular.

The party lasted until 2 a.m. The men had alcohol to

keep them going; the women lasted on high spirits alone – becoming intoxicated would be most immodest. When most of the guests had left, the remaining, unmarried boys were ushered to one end of the hall and told not to look while our family members sat in two rows, men opposite women. A lone keyboard player struck up as a guest, pre-designated for this well-trodden tradition, launched into limericks about each relative. He addressed each man in turn, climbing the familial hierarchy to Danny's father, then mine, then Danny last, as, one by one, they each danced with me, each grasping the end of a woven silk belt so as not to touch hands. I was married now and expected to do no more than sway, barely, to the music while they performed. When it reached Daddy's turn, he threw the belt aside, took my hand and danced, crying. He'd had so many expectations of me, of this moment, and for the first time I think I met them. All I could do now was begin my next act.

7

You're not righteous, you're stupid

מִדְּבַר־שֶׁקֶר תִּרְחָק

Keep far away from anything to do with falsehood.

Exodus 23:7

We went home to a grotty flat on the second floor of an ex-council block in Hackney, which I'd seen only once before – to arrange some of my clothes and put my knickers in a drawer earlier that week. I'd found the rest of my clothes already waiting for me there, altered for modesty, steamed and put away by Mrs Blau. Mrs Blau was there to mentor both of us now, but hers and mine was a strange relationship; she would buy me clothes she thought Danny would like and arrange beauty appointments for me, yet it never seemed like she was happy for us.

It was almost morning at the end of our wedding night, and Danny sat down in front of the computer in the study where he'd hung up his new husband clothes: a fur *shtreimel* hat to replace the black Homburg he wore on *shabbos* and an overcoat called a *rezvulke beketshe* that denoted status by virtue of marriage. I went to the bathroom, wriggled out of my dress and showered. I changed into a flimsy black nightie and black satin dressing gown that I'd chosen together with Peninah, who I trusted to know what appropriate wedding night lingerie looked like, despite neither of us ever having been married. When I emerged, I lay down on the bed, on my back, and looked to Danny, who was hovering awkwardly. He didn't know where to put himself so I turned off the light and beckoned for him to lie beside me. He said he wanted to shower first and came back a few minutes later in a floor-length Burberry robe tied in a neat knot under his belly.

He joined me on the bed but he wasn't quite hard. We kissed and I opened my legs and showed him where to put it. I felt nothing – only that I was serving G-d by doing what needed to be done.

When he came, Danny recoiled in horror and jumped off the bed, grabbed his robe and held it in front of him as I watched his bottom retreat to the bathroom. The marriage was consummated now and Danny wouldn't be allowed to touch me until I'd had my period and immersed in the *mikveh* again. We went to sleep in separated beds, to come together again in a fortnight.

Our wedding night was a Sunday. The following Friday was the first time he showed me his temper. I had two *sheitel*s. The first, my fancy one, was the wig styled for the wedding. The second was an everyday one, soft, brown and shoulder-length with a little fringe that swept to one side. I wore this for each of the seven nights after our wedding, when friends and family threw *Sheva Brachos* – or seven blessings – a week of parties in people's homes to bestow blessings on our marriage. *Shabbos* was the most special of these. On Friday morning, Mrs Blau called to say she would collect me to visit her *sheitel macher* (wig maker). This wasn't the lady who'd prepared and cut my wigs for my wedding and my marriage in her basement; Mrs Blau's lady had the most luxurious wigs I had ever seen, arranged in a rather luxe salon attached to her home.

'I've discussed your face and style, and we've decided what would be best for you,' announced Mrs Blau when we arrived. She had already taken me for laser treatment, before the wedding, to burn away the widow's peak at the top of my hairline lest, she said, it poke out immodestly from under my wig. Unbeknown to me, she had, since the wedding, taken my fancy wig to be restyled and I was presented with a shoulder-length replacement, ironed straight and arranged so that it was away from my face.

When I got home, Danny hated it. Without speaking, he picked up the phone to Mrs Blau and furiously told her in Yiddish: 'I'm embarrassed to walk with her in the street.'

He spoke to her as though he was bursting with dissatisfaction, incensed that I'd exposed him by giving him something to be angry about. I could hear her trying to talk him down on the other end of the line and was struck by how strange their tone was with one another, as though she knew this side of him already. Why was he asking her to fix something that was between us?

As they talked about me, I looked at my reflection in the mirror and touched the wig on the stranger looking back. My heart raced. Not even a week after my wedding I was already wondering, *How the fuck do I get out of this entire situation?*

Danny passed me the phone and Mrs Blau told me I was to wear a white scarf on top of my wig, a change she believed would make Danny happier: it would make me look more pious at our *shabbos* celebration, which was being hosted by friends that night at a local banqueting hall.

Mrs Blau sent a driver to take us there but Danny was still tense when we arrived. I got out of my side of the car and he got out of his, accidentally trapping his hand in the door as he slammed it shut. Still out of sight of others, he lost his cool. He swore at me and sweated, red in the face. I felt a pit form in my stomach as I saw my husband's true nature. I had married a pressure cooker and it frightened me. I walked in alone, leaving him on the pavement behind me, to follow.

From then on, I wore a proverbial mask, always trying to keep my image right and plot my next move. His temper came out frequently, triggered by the smallest things: if I bought food or cooked a meal or wore something he didn't like. In April, we went to the USA on a long, extravagant honeymoon visiting Niagara Falls, Miami, the Bahamas and New York over two and a half weeks. We didn't have sex once; he didn't even try, which confused me, given that it was the only thing I'd been taught to provide for him. Sometimes, he even requested separate rooms for us, which left me feeling discarded. I didn't have my own money or phone, which meant I was essentially stuck. For the final leg of our trip, we stayed in a five-star hotel in the centre of Manhattan. Danny was either in bed, sullen, inattentive and distant, or on his own at a casino. I really wanted to see a Broadway show and tried to convince him we'd have fun but he wasn't interested and it sparked an argument.

In a flight of frustration I said I'd go without him and

turned to leave. Before I could get to the door he reached for my handbag, hung across my body, and suddenly, sharply, pulled the strap tight around my neck. He pushed me on to the bed and crossed the strap into an X around my throat. All I could think of was my breath. It felt a hundred miles away yet, at the same time, right there. I needed to reach it. I struggled against him and scratched his face with my nails, drawing blood. Surprised, he let up for a moment. That was all I needed – I sat up, yanked the receiver off the room phone and dialled zero for the front desk.

'My husband is beating me,' I said clearly, almost flat, trying to keep myself alive. Danny knew when to quit. He backed off entirely and sank down into the velvet armchair by the window, nursing his face.

Moments later, two security guards knocked on our door, asking to come in. They sat down and looked at us both. They had called the police, who soon arrived, chewing gum and cracking jokes. They called me 'ma'am' but Danny was the only one with a visible wound, so it was me they'd have to take to the station, they explained. I looked at them in disbelief. In the mirror I could see my neck, blooming purple, from his hands.

'That's just a bruise,' they said. Realizing that there was no winner in this situation, we agreed to press no charges and they promptly left.

I saw Danny's phone on the dressing table, forgotten in all the chaos, and tucked it into the waistband of my skirt. Desperate for help, I went into the bathroom and called the only person who I could think of to talk him down: Mrs Blau. I stood with my back against the bathroom door and told her how his temper had flared again. Before I could even finish, he stormed in and slammed me against the marble counter. My hips felt like they had shattered. My screams were so loud that the cleaning staff outside our room heard and called security back. Danny was escorted off the premises and a Chasidic man who had pulled up in a luxury SUV car bustled into the lobby, calling out my name.

'Mrs Blau has arranged for me to take you down Fifth Avenue and said to give you spending money,' he explained, leading me out of the hotel.

I followed because I really didn't know what else to do. He delivered me to a small kosher hotel in Borough Park, the Chasidic neighbourhood closest to Manhattan, where my luggage was already in the room. 'I'll pick you up at 5 a.m. for your flight home,' he said. I put my bags at the end of the single bed and checked my neck to see if the bruising was visible above the high collar of my jumper before going downstairs for dinner. I sat alone at a table for two, trying to get my head around the past twenty-four hours. That night, I barely slept. Instead, my mind raced back and forth between that familiar feeling of not knowing what would happen to me next and wondering when I would have to see Danny again.

When I arrived at the airport the following morning, there he was, standing at the boarding gate. Far from being held in the cells, I later found out he'd spent the night in Atlantic City. He didn't make eye contact with me as we waited for our flight home. When it was time, we sat down in the business-class seats he'd booked before we left England, facing away from one another as anxiety gripped me from the inside out.

Back in London, the tension continued to escalate. Danny

wouldn't let me buy food for the house. Instead, he wanted us to eat in the proper Chasidic way, which is, for the first year, to be fed by our families. The idea was to relieve newly-wed teenagers of domestic responsibilities, but our version was extreme. Most nights, we'd go to his parents' for supper. I couldn't drive; most Chasidic families follow teachings that consider it improper for women to learn and neither my father, nor Danny, had given permission for that so he'd drive us every time. Every so often, Mrs Blau would take me shopping to Harvey Nichols and Selfridges and dress me, like a doll. I'd married into opulence yet, at home, I'd resorted to stealing from a jar of coins Danny kept on his desk to buy myself a tuna sandwich at lunchtime. I could not grasp what my life had become.

Mrs Blau arranged a job for me (I'd left the ones I had in Gateshead to get married in London). The new role was four days a week, in another travel agency that catered for Chasidic customers. The proprietor's wife was a kind woman who started every day by checking the *Hello!* magazine website, and her father, who had been a prisoner in Bergen-Belsen concentration camp, would visit daily with bread, milk and the joy of life. The camaraderie was amazing and I relished the hours I spent there, but I had to go home at the end of each day.

By the beginning of June, Danny wasn't going to work any more. He had been doing insurance stuff but now he spent every day in bed watching box sets, which was definitely sinful. Television did not advance Torah learning and was therefore an impious use of time. A lot of homes didn't have a television at all but Danny at least chose his shows well. I'd join him watching *The Sopranos* and *24* when I got in from work to our house with no food.

One day, I came home earlier than expected. I opened the bedroom door to find Danny leaning back against the pillows – and Mrs Blau by the bed, tucking her blouse into her tights; she wasn't wearing a skirt. I looked at them both. He didn't move. She stood there and looked back at me.

'Oh my god, I'm so sorry,' I said, the apology rushing out as I shut my own bedroom door behind me.

I went into the living room, closed the door and began pacing. What the hell was my life? I waited for the sound of our front door to shut behind her then returned to the bedroom. I didn't ask what had happened – that was quite clear; instead I asked 'Where is she?', confirming that she'd gone. And that was it. It was never spoken about again, by either of them. I never caught them again but it was quietly obvious to us all that it wasn't the first time and it wouldn't be the last.

Danny and I were both lost kids. Mrs Blau had already inserted herself into our lives in a way that made her the only person who could help me, just as she had helped Danny for years before I'd arrived. She was the hand that both gave and took away. I felt both humiliated, suddenly in competition with her yet, at the same time, oddly vindicated. The oddness of our new marriage suddenly made sense. Though she and Danny might have been having sex, we rarely did. What bothered me more than the betrayal, what hurt me, was how far I was from the legitimacy that came with a functioning marriage, a protective husband and motherhood. 'Please G-d,' I'd pray each month when I visited the *mikveh*, hoping for all those things. 'Please G-d, help him come to me.'

The High Holidays were terrible that year. This spate of festivals begins each autumn with Rosh Hashanah, the Jewish new year, then Yom Kippur, the Day of Atonement, and ends with Simchat Torah, when we celebrate the annual conclusion of the Torah readings and restart the scroll. Danny and I were invited to Leah's but Danny didn't want to go. When I threatened to go alone, he said: 'If you go, you're not coming back.'

I went to Leah's anyway, broken. I told her what had happened between Danny and Mrs Blau and stayed with her for a week. My family went into panic mode and it was decided – by the same people who had sat around the table when we got engaged – that I should go back to my flat and talk to my husband. We agreed to try again. We even had sex that night but I already knew, from the mad, desperate look in his eyes, that it was never going to work.

I wasn't stupid. The pre-ordained life that had been offered to me as a solution to all my problems was in reality just another problem. I needed to consider my future and began getting my affairs in order. I gave my wedding jewellery to Mrs Blau, hoping she could trade them in for me; it was worth at least £10,000, which was going to be more valuable to me than diamonds. When he discovered it had gone, Danny came looking for me. I was on the phone, in the kitchen. He tackled me on to the floor. I screamed as he held me down, the weight of his body flattening me beneath him, his hands like cuffs around my wrists. I pushed and kicked myself free, and banged with all my might on the window. I stared as jagged lines grew in front of me, mesmerized by my own strength, then the glass smashed. For a moment, I felt a power I didn't recognize.

The flats were built around a courtyard and Danny clocked that neighbours were now looking in. He let go of me.

'What do you want?' he asked, breathless.

'Just let me walk out the door,' I said, never clearer.

He unlocked the front door. I knocked on a neighbour's and asked to use their phone. They'd heard it all and let me in, no questions. I called Leah, walked twenty minutes to hers and never saw Danny again.

Despite the community's stance on divorce, wives walking out in those situations was not uncommon. Not walking back in, however, was more unusual.

Our marriage had lasted nine months. Three months after I had left, I received my *get* – a religious divorce authorized by the Beth Din. But there was a condition attached. Among the reasons I had given was what I'd walked in on between Danny and Mrs Blau. Mrs Blau was an important and wealthy member of the community. She wielded power and protection. The Beth Din wouldn't agree to it unless I retracted what I'd told them about her.

I was handed a piece of paper, written in Hebrew, to sign. It read: 'Everything that I said and thought against the important woman Mrs Henna Blau, may she live long and be well, was from the heat and bitterness of my heart. There's no truth in there at all, not even a little bit of truth. Rather, the person we are speaking about did a lot of good for me and I can never repay her . . . I hope that she forgives me.'

If I signed, I would get £10,000 and the divorce, but I told the adjudicator I didn't want to tell a lie.

'You're not righteous,' he said, in Hebrew. 'You're stupid.'

I knew I had to sign but I could distance myself from the

lie, too. I wrote out my married name, Yehudis Horowitz, knowing full well that I had never changed any identification documents from Fletcher. This was the only piece of paper in existence to bear that name. The person who signed it wasn't me.

8

Divorced, engaged

וַיֹּאמֶר יְהוָה אֱלֹהִים לֹא־טוֹב הֱיוֹת הָאָדָם לְבַדּוֹ אֶעֱשֶׂה־לּוֹ עֵזֶר כְּנֶגְדּוֹ

G-d said, 'It is not good for the Human to be alone; I will make a fitting counterpart for him.'

Genesis 2:18

THE RACE WAS ON TO prove that the collapse of my marriage hadn't been my fault. I was a nineteen-year-old divorcee and my parents, despite having been ambivalent to the circumstances of my split, needed a second husband to take me off their hands.

'Oh, Yehudis, what have you been and gone and done?' my mother would say, in the same exacerbated tone she used when I told my schoolfriends what sex was.

Leah offered me a room in her home, despite already being a mother to six children, and I contributed a minimal amount of rent. I still had my job and some disposable income. In the evenings, I hung out with Peninah, and other single friends who hadn't married yet. Peninah had her provisional driving licence and we'd take her mother's car out for joy rides. I was keen to learn to drive but my brother-in-law forbade it: 'Not while you're living under my roof,' he'd say. With any spare money I bought myself clothes and, having had a taste of luxury on Mrs Blau's shopping trips, cultivated a look I considered chic: A-line skirts that fell to just above the knee, paired with soft cashmere jumpers. My hair had to stay covered – there was no return to girlhood in that regard – so I saved up and bought myself a new wig – softer, longer, sexier.

I spent a lot of time in the attic room at Leah's, secretly scrolling on my BlackBerry. Web access is banned outright by Chasidic leadership; the sheer availability of information is deemed too dangerous, too frightening. Non-Jewish ideas are strictly forbidden but there is a tacit acceptance that the internet is necessary for email communication, banking and travel sites – important factors when transporting growing families across the globe to attend each other's life events. By this token, my father, as a rabbi, had a desktop computer at home, and the potential of this rich information resource had been fascinating to me. Now that I finally had my own means of accessing the internet, I found my way to Hashkafa.com, a forum that invited Jewish people to discuss philosophical ideas originating from religious texts. The site existed in the grey area between permissible and forbidden. I found the discussion threads stimulating in a world where women were not meant to be stimulated. I'd only ever been told that questioning G-d was wrong, but here I discovered a community who found joy in getting to grips with the theology of it all. I was like a parched wanderer being led to water and relished the hours I spent engaged in deep, questioning conversations there.

The other thing that occupied my time in the attic was watching the sitcom *Will & Grace*. Penina, the friend who'd smuggled *DIVA* magazines to Gateshead for me, secretly gave me a portable DVD player and a shopping bag containing every season of the show. I watched with headphones in, under the duvet, until 2 a.m., enjoying my screen-size view of a world beyond the one I knew.

One night, Leah knocked on the door, late. I stuffed the player under my bed and let her in. She was excited.

'A *shidduch* has come up,' she whispered. 'The man who suggested it is downstairs. Get dressed and come down.'

I put on a modest housecoat and followed Leah downstairs, where a friendly man who seemed to have the joy of G-d inside him was propped up against the breakfast bar in the kitchen. I stood on the other side as he told me about his American cousin, Zvi.

'He's a little different,' he explained.

Zvi was from the Satmar community in New York, the world's largest Chasidic dynasty, but he didn't wear a *shtreimel* – the wide-brimmed fur hat that its men favoured. This was uncouth of him and, Zvi hoped, made us alike. He was interested in the essence of G-d but not the externalization of it, which seemed an OK start. Perhaps, like me, I thought, he could see that there was some way to observe and enjoy your faith without subscribing to every single rule.

They'd summoned me because Zvi was currently on a tour

of holy men's graves in Eastern Europe – a recognized, male-centric phenomenon for someone who needed a religious reset. He would be in London very briefly the following week before returning to Brooklyn, so there was only a narrow window for us to meet.

The next day, my brother-in-law reported that Zvi had requested a photo of me. I adjusted my wig and posed against the living room wall, wearing a baby-pink buttoned-up blouse. No one offered me a photo of Zvi.

The following week, I found myself once again sat at Leah's table as I was introduced to another husband, nineteen months after the first. I felt like a false, flat, smaller version of myself. It was déjà vu and with it came a sense of defeat.

Zvi was exceptionally short, 5ft 3ins, with a trimmed ginger beard and heavy moustache. He was very stocky, very nervous and very sweaty. He was twenty-nine, ten years older than me, and he too had been married once before.

He seemed so grateful to be there. I looked at him and thought: *He's* not going to hit me.

He picked me up in a taxi the next day. 'I paid the driver 50p extra to open the door for you,' he said as he twisted round from the front seat. We were driven to a Hilton hotel, where we sat in the lobby and drank orange juice. He didn't stop talking. I couldn't keep track of the family members whose names he was reeling off at speed, so I stayed quiet. He didn't seem to mind. Zvi had a kind face and a hovering, nervous demeanour. He wasn't sexy to me. I resigned myself to the fact this was the best I was going to get; unless I could find a direct reason not to, I ought to get on with it.

We met again, at his cousin's house, a couple of days later.

His *cappel* was folded in half on his head, his trousers hung too low and he looked dishevelled. No part of me found him attractive, but it still hadn't occurred to me that it was a factor of any importance. I messed about with serviettes under the table while he talked. By Sunday, there were cakes set out in Leah's dining room once again and my mother was there. Zvi told me my shirt button was undone and it was showing my collarbone; she loved the fact he corrected me on that. Finally, someone to pick up the baton of keeping me on the straight and narrow.

We sat down at the table, Zvi flanked by his cousin and my brother-in-law, me by my mother and Leah, and no one spoke.

'OK,' I said. 'Are we going to do this?'

He remained silent and prayed heartfelt thanks to the Lord for our unspoken engagement. I didn't know what to do, so I stood up. My mother was glowing. *Mazel tov*s were said and his parents called from the States. I feigned a wide smile that made my cheeks ache. Everything was back on track. How wonderful.

That night there was a party, smaller than the first time round because of course we didn't want to normalize divorce or suggest you could do it all again with no impact. Men gathered in Leah's front room, women in the narrow galley kitchen. The breakfast bar was piled high with cakes. I wore a chocolate-brown silk jacket and matching skirt from Monsoon, chocolate-brown kitten heels and nude tights. Elegant. No part of me felt I was being made a fuss of, but then no one was expecting me to enjoy myself – I just had to show up and I knew how to do that by now. A message came from the men that my groom wanted to speak to me outside. I walked out of the front door, where the party was spilling into the street and a stereo was blasting from an ancient Toyota. It was as though the cool guys from the neighbourhood had come to see the spectacle that was Yehudis Fletcher's second engagement.

I found Zvi by the gatepost. 'What do you want?' I asked him.

'I'm having a cigarette,' he said. 'I just wanted you to keep me company.'

I didn't have anything meaningful to say to him. We talked about who was there, what was happening inside. Then, I looked down and noticed a tent at his crotch. Flustered, he excused himself and headed back inside. I was left on the pavement feeling nauseous. There was absolutely nothing appealing about that to me but it served as a reminder of what was going to be expected from me again. I had to put it out of my mind to get down the aisle.

The wedding was five weeks later. There was no buzz of anticipation in the way there was for my first wedding. A second wedding is like a game of snakes and ladders: I'd slid down a snake, now I had to climb back up the ladder and reinstate my status as a married woman.

The ceremony took place in a room above a Blockbuster video-rental shop, forty-five minutes away, that was rented out as function space to a local synagogue. It was June 2007. There was no fuss like last time. I got ready in the attic at Leah's and went through all the same purity prep but this time without a chaperone; I knew what to do. I pulled on a new wig. This time I'd chosen one that was a little longer than the one I'd worn in my previous marriage. My dress was off-white satin with a beaded bodice, which I wore with flat white Mary Janes from Primark. My make-up was understated and a friend of mine came round to help me apply it. My father-in-law wanted me to wear the heavy veil but my mother objected. 'She's not a virgin bride,' she said.

My parents travelled in the car with me. There were no more than fifty guests – family and a handful of friends. The tables were set but there were no flowers this time. The room looked just the way it did on *shabbos*, when congregants gathered to break bread after the service. The *chuppah* was inside because you don't draw attention to a second wedding by having it in public. There was no *yichud* room for us to spend our first private moments as husband and wife so, as though it were entirely normal, we were sent to the next-door building, where a family had vacated their home for us.

Inside our makeshift *yichud*, I felt him walk up behind me. He put his hands on my waist, then pulled my head round to face him and kissed me, his tongue everywhere. Still gripping me, he sat down and pulled me on to his lap.

'My teacher told me to do it that way,' he said. I was quiet.

When we returned next door for photographs, he continued to grope me as I smiled for the camera. Meanwhile, there was dissatisfaction brewing among some of our guests, who deemed the decision to serve salmon and chicken on the same plate unkosher and unfit to eat. I took my seat next to Grandma G and looked at her. We both knew this was a shitshow.

Zvi spent much of the evening telling people he couldn't

wait to get home and have sex with me. In the car on the way back, he started saying the prayers that were to be recited before sex so as not to waste time once we were over the threshold. I was terrified at the thought of doing this again.

We walked down five, steep steps into the dingy basement flat we were renting in Stamford Hill. The front door opened straight into its only room, which contained a galley kitchen and dining room table, with a partition marking out a bedroom with two single beds. I showered in the small bathroom by the front door and put on a pair of pink-and-rose-gold-striped satin pyjamas. Zvi showered next and emerged in a navy bathrobe. He had sex with me five times that night and got up in the middle to make popcorn. I was numb in every single way, every cell permeated by the sensation of nothingness.

In the days after, he didn't stop. The sex was constant. With Danny, we had pretended that I hadn't been abused and followed the cycle of purity laws that virgin newlyweds would; there was no pretence with Zvi, no official need to wait until my next period was over, so he just kept going. In bridal lessons, which I'd now had two bouts of with the same teacher, I was taught that saying 'no' to sex was an option but would have its consequences. If I were to refuse my husband, he might then go to a prostitute or, worse still, masturbate, rendering the babies that his sperm might have turned into dead because of me.

And so, I had to make the best of the situation. I tried to find moments of connection with this man who was having sex with me that I did not find enjoyable. I'd crack jokes and clean myself up again and again in this tiny space, sometimes without enough time to finish washing before he'd try again. I was sore, desperate, and tired.

There were no *Sheva Brachos* this time, nothing to ease the newlyweds into domestic life. We were on our own. Three or four mornings in, after yet another round of fucking, he pulled out to reveal his white Y-fronts red with my blood. I had taken myself so out of my own body by this point that I couldn't even feel pain. I called my mother and asked her what to do. Obviously I needed to go to A&E but she insisted I mustn't. That would take it outside the community. Instead I called a religious GP's wife who lived locally and asked to see her husband. We walked to their home, around the corner, and he asked me to lie down on the couch in their living room, where he examined me and confirmed that the blood was from a tear to my perineum and wasn't cyclical. 'Next time put a cushion under her bottom,' he told Zvi. As soon as the bleeding stopped, a day or two later, he continued. I got a two-week reprieve only when my next period arrived. Within six weeks I was pregnant.

9

Mumsnet

נֶאֱמָנִים פִּצְעֵי אוֹהֵב וְנַעְתָּרוֹת נְשִׁיקוֹת שׂוֹנֵא

Wounds by a loved one are long-lasting; the kisses of an enemy are profuse.

Proverbs 27:5–6

MOTHERHOOD WAS THE THING I'D been striving for since before I met Danny but my striving was a mechanical one, not a yearning. My belly was my ticket to acceptability. Aged twenty, it made me the same as all the other young brides walking around Stamford Hill with their babies in Bugaboo pushchairs. It bought me approval – or, at the very least, a lack of criticism.

Talking about pregnancy would tempt the devil so it wasn't something to be publicly celebrated until the baby arrived. We quietly prepared in our tiny flat. The nightmare for me was that with the absence of periods I was always clean; I had nothing to keep me away from my obligations to Zvi.

I was anxious throughout the pregnancy. I was either

worried that I'd lose the baby or plagued by the fear that I would be an unfit mother. I'd seen how wrung out my sisters were after their babies arrived and, worse still, had this torturous narrative in my head that abused people turn into abusers. As my nerves mounted, we made plans to give up our flat and move into Leah's a few weeks before my due date, staying there for a while once the baby was born.

I was anxious about the birth, too. In my final month of pregnancy, I visited a lady in the community who invited expectant mothers into her living room and explained how to breathe during labour, but beyond that there was nothing else to prepare me. Women weren't meant to share details of their births, so other than a general gist, I had no clue what awaited me. I went into labour on the evening of Sunday 18 May. We took a cab to Homerton Hospital, taking a religious doula with us to navigate the culture clash, as was customary. She was a demure lady on the rota of women who volunteered for this work and the birth rate in communities like ours meant demand was high. She tied her headscarf in the most modest way possible, with no hairline on show, and had sour breath that she exhaled on to my face while offering me lollipops to suck on as I laboured.

'Yes! Yes!' she encouraged in her American accent. 'With every pain you should feel Hashem's [G-d's] light shine upon you.'

I had no context for this pain. Was it supposed to feel this way or was something terribly wrong? I was lost in it and high on gas and air. My midwife was a kind West African lady who spoke in a calming voice and whose wig was slightly askew. I crawled around on my hands and knees as

I pushed, struggling and scared. She took care of me gently, wiping me clean and coaxing me to keep going.

Zvi was praying in the corridor, so as not to see me undressed while impure, as I was deemed from the moment my waters broke. It was 7 a.m. and I'd been in labour all night by the time they got me on to the bed, then with one final horrific push, I gave birth to a boy, a tiny red scrap, born screaming. The midwife passed him to me. I held him for a moment then handed him back. I don't even remember looking at his face. I felt the same way I'd felt the first night Todros assaulted me. Absent. Violated. Zvi fainted when the baby was handed to him, and my sisters arrived and gushed over how cute he was. Mentally, I was somewhere else.

We called him Noam. He was beautiful, tiny, weightless, but I couldn't enjoy that through the haze. At eight days old, he had his *bris*, the ritual circumcision that every Jewish man has had since Abraham; a sign of his covenant with G-d. It was usual for this to take place at home and my parents joined us from Israel, cooing over the baby. I stayed upstairs. I was in agony from a tear that had been stitched up improperly and become infected and, mentally, I was growing more and more distant and tortured by the trauma of birth and my past.

At Leah's, there were now more than a dozen people living under one roof and it was painfully clear we were taking up too much space. We argued over everything, from the number of buggies – hers and mine – crowding the hallway, to when visitors were allowed. When Noam was twelve days old, Leah found me space in a local mothers' recuperation home and Zvi's uncle offered to pay. In these homes, new mothers are provided with three hot meals a day and the babies are looked after in a nursery and brought to you when they need feeding. Bearing in mind some women have babies every year, it had the feel of a holiday camp – an annual retreat for relaxation and renewal before it was time to go home and have another baby.

This particular one was in a nondescript brick building, the inside of which looked like a care home. There were a dozen bedrooms and the focal point was the breastfeeding room, which was like a lounge with tall, wipe-clean armchairs and breastfeeding cushions, just off the nursery. I spent my days in a zip-up robe and Zvi visited daily in a state of unhelpful panic. Officially, we didn't have shelter and I was too preoccupied with new motherhood to pay attention to where he was staying the rest of the time or to be in any rush to leave. At peace in the recuperation home, the women shared baby stories and laughed together, and it brought me joy every day.

On the inside, however, bigger things were going on. Noam was so little, and I was terrified I was going to hurt him. Trying to extinguish this thought took every ounce of my strength when I tended to him. The fear that somehow I would one day become just like the monster of my past was all-consuming. When I left, eleven days later, Leah's husband had found a barely habitable house for us to rent diagonally across the road from them. There was no hot water or heating but it was summer, at least, and not too cold. There was a microwave and a single saucepan, which I used to boil water for formula because I wasn't making enough milk. I'd sterilize the bottles, heat the water, and repeat all day and night. I'd slipped a disc while I was in the recuperation home so I'd crawl up the stairs, lie the baby next to me and cry, existing only through pain and exhaustion.

The midwife would visit and ask how we were doing, and I'd tell her: 'I feel suicidal.'

'Oh, it looks like you're OK,' she'd reply and fill out her forms.

We were sustained by a freezer full of kosher hospital meals that someone had bought at cost price. We didn't feel like the family unit I'd grown up imagining at all. I felt completely, increasingly alone and absolutely terrified. I'd wait for Zvi to come home from work before I bathed Noam so there was someone else there. I saw myself as an abuse victim and therefore automatic perpetrator, someone who needed constant surveillance, rather than a fit mother. The days where I was alone with the baby stretched out into long, agonizing hours of fear and self-doubt. When he was a month old and my back pain hadn't subsided, I asked Zvi to drive me to A&E to try to get help. The hospital managed to help me with my physical ailments, but hadn't clocked that my psychological health was much worse; I was borderline psychotic. I wandered out of the hospital and stood in the middle of the road mumbling to myself, before Zvi bundled me into a car and took me home.

He was working as a bookkeeper at the time and six weeks into fatherhood, with less sex available at home on account of me being impure in my postpartum state, he felt that being stuck in an office alone with a female co-worker wasn't appropriate, without what Talmudists call *pas besalo* – bread in his basket – that is, a wife as a receptacle for any urges he may have had.

So, in the worst mental state of my life, I was back at work four days a week, leaving my baby with Zvi's aunt. No one at work seemed to think this was a problem, or that the suggested solution was strange. 'You're only here because Zvi was on heat,' said my new boss a few weeks in. It was humiliating. Everyone in the office knew that I was there because of my husband's libido. But it was my responsibility to manage our marriage. I didn't feel as though I had a choice.

Miraculously, the enforced regimen of going into the office made motherhood fall into place for me. I went from an endless blur of tear-filled days spent heating freezer food and sterilizing bottles to a more functional routine that gave us some structure. I'd fill the slow cooker each morning before I left, drop off the baby and settle down at my desk, enjoying the reprieve of a quiet office and adult conversation. The responsibility of meeting both my son's and husband's needs forced me to dig deep to keep all three of us going, and with time and sleep I began to realize that I was getting us through each day, over and over again. I began to see myself as a mother and to trust myself with my little boy.

I learned that motherhood could be a route to relative freedom: pushing a buggy was like going out with a shield, whereby people's eyes focused on the baby, not me. With Noam, I enjoyed being out and about in the community more than I ever had before. He was an adorable child, curious and alert, and he provided a new, safe topic of conversation for other people to engage with. I felt I had renewed purpose within my family. Doing things the way people expected me to and achieving the status I had so craved elevated my sense of belonging considerably. While I was still far from confident in motherhood, I started to believe that I could do what everyone around me was doing. I could be the 'woman of valour' that I wanted to be, G-d wanted me to be and that my parents had always hoped I could be.

Noam was six months old when a friend introduced me to another kind of freedom: vibrators. Sexual pleasure was new to me. It had never been taught or discussed except for in marriage lessons, where I was told it was a *mitzvah* – a good deed – to fulfil my husband's need for it. I had heard of a female orgasm, but it felt completely disconnected from the advice I'd been given to pretend to enjoy sex if I wanted to get it over with quicker. Zvi had been fretting to his family about my apparently too-low sex drive, prompting my sister-in-law to encourage homeopathic remedies to improve it, but I found my own way. I was sitting on my friend Ruchy's sofa, discussing the problem over a glass of wine while the baby slept in his pram, when she showed me a massive, pink, silicone rabbit. I'd heard of them, but never seen or touched one before. She told me it would be good for me and ordered me one. It was battery-operated, so I couldn't use it on *shabbos*, but I found a rhythm in using the short window when Zvi left for *shul* on a Friday night, before *shabbos* came in – the same window my mother used to put her feet up on the space heater – to enjoy a quick orgasm before I lit the candles.

Ruchy and I had known each other for a number of years. She wasn't my closest friend but she seemed to notice my struggle to adjust to married life. She wasn't in an easy situation herself, with two very young children and a husband who treated her horrendously, but she saw that I needed a hand getting to know myself outside of my marriage. I never told her anything explicit but she sensed that I needed friendship and, most of all, a girls' night out. A few weeks later, she suggested we go to Candy Bar, a lesbian club on Carlisle Street in Soho. She recommended it, not because of its gay clientele but on the basis that it was all women and thus somewhat modest. We put our babies to bed and explained our plans to our respective husbands, who were unphased, given there would be no other men there. If anything, they felt gallant, cool even, by letting us go. We took the Tube into Soho; I wore my wig but hoped I looked otherwise inconspicuous, with a modest but stylish all-black outfit. We turned into the grimy, narrow doorway, got our hands stamped and walked into three floors of women and pop music.

The sea of women in front of me pulsated with power and I wanted to borrow from it. The last time I'd danced among women was at my wedding. There, I had felt their joy; here I felt my own. That evening was the first time I'd faced my own sexuality since before I was married. If what the rabbi said was true, I should have long been rid of any lesbian desires, but in the darkness of the club I now knew they were still there. I was so afraid of how attracted I was to everyone. Ruchy started dancing right away, but I leaned against the wall, taking it all in. It took only a moment before people smelled fresh meat and came to say hello. Some were welcoming. One, a hot, petite South Asian woman about my age, with perfect skin, cropped hair and dark, thick-framed glasses, was fascinated by my wig and asked me to dance. I said 'no', scared of the heat I felt when I looked at her. She bought me a drink, then another, until I was feeling drunk enough to be playful. I took the frames from her face and tried them on, enjoying the transient contact of my fingertips against her cheekbones. By the time I told her I was leaving, we'd been dancing for over two hours. It was around midnight. She pulled me back in and kissed me, long and hard.

'OK, now you can go,' she said.

My body turned to liquid.

This experience was like dousing water over hot coals; it provided both relief and ignited the realization that I was someone different from the life I was living. It made me look at the world outside my community as something not to be shunned but to be hacked; navigating it could help me to work out how much more I wanted and how much I had to lose. The baby was my pass out of there. Sure, I didn't take him to lesbian nightclubs, but I began using him as an excuse to travel beyond Stamford Hill, taking him on buses and the Tube to free museums and parks where I could watch other versions of life pass by.

I continued working in the office with Zvi. I worked hard. I was respected and I climbed in the estimations of my peers while he sat back, lacking the impetus to do the same. By the time Noam was sixteen months old, we had moved to Edgware, where there was a smaller and less isolated Charedi community, on the outskirts of north London. I was pregnant for the second time. This pregnancy was easier, now I knew what to expect, and with a second child on the way, I was settling into my role as wife and mother. One of the first things to occupy my mind was what I could do to ensure this birth was different from Noam's. I typed 'How can I have a good birth?' into Google on my BlackBerry, and came across a website called Mumsnet.

If the big twenty-first-century sin is using the internet to access non-Jewish ideas, an even bigger sin is discussing them with strangers online. I did both. I joined the community of mothers and commented frequently on their posts about their husbands' indiscretions, annoying mothers-in-law, household budgeting and recipes. I had an annoying mother-in-law and recipes for soup, too. It was a view into other women's lives but I could relate. I chose the username Mrs Micawber, after the tired and overwhelmed wife in Dickens's *David Copperfield*, and picked up the lingo, learning to identify a 'stealth boast' when I saw one and telling other women to LTB (leave the bastard). Naturally, I was some way off fitting in there but I loved the camaraderie. It reminded me of the women in my community, but without the narrow constraints on conversation. I could fit a whole other world in my pocket.

When Noam had chickenpox, I asked the other Mumsnetters why I had received odd looks when I took him on the bus. In my community, no one was taught the science of mass contamination and I thought the other passengers had been rude, passing judgement on my child's appearance. Online, the Mumsnetters came for me. How could I be so selfish? How could I risk other people's health that way? I didn't know what they were talking about. I received their wholesale condemnation and mockery but I enjoyed the challenge. I was used to being told what not to do so it wasn't enough to put me off. Quite the opposite, I was enthralled by what I was learning about the world. When we booked a flight to visit Zvi's family in New York, I asked for ideas to keep a toddler entertained on a long journey. One user suggested toy dinosaurs. 'He loves figurines but unfortunately we don't believe in dinosaurs,' I replied.

On 7 December 2010, my second child was born – a girl, Talia. Mumsnet had taught me how to ask for better support during birth and it had educated me on how to bond more with my baby, including buying a sling to carry her around in. With the support of a different, better doula, I did squats in the hospital corridor as we willed my waters to break. Talia was born blue and didn't cry. When the doctors resuscitated her and placed her in my arms, her tiny, perfect lips seemed to smile up at me. I thought she was beautiful. There was a difference in me.

I spent a week at the recuperation home with her. Though I was in an altogether more positive place than last time, when we went home, I still cried. The task ahead is daunting to all new mothers. But I had a little family now and I had grown to feel deeply connected to my children. I had worked through my earlier fears and knew that I was a good mother to Noam. I would be a good mother to Talia, too.

Noam was clever, chatting away and learning the alphabet from toys and puzzles. Talia was quieter, and I wore her in a sling just as Mumsnet had suggested. I took her to work with me from six weeks while Noam went to his childminder and we continued the routine until she was eight months old, when I started to leave her with a babysitter.

I was becoming more and more capable, while Zvi was struggling to manage the household. For Jewish holidays or *shabbos*, I'd invite at least two other families over. I enjoyed having others to talk to. On Sunday afternoons, Zvi would take Noam to the nearby city farm so I could rest with Talia. We'd fallen into a new functioning routine but I struggled to feel any closeness with my husband, who still wanted sex all the time.

As I learned more about what I wanted, I found him increasingly off-putting and, thanks to Mumsnet, I had a rising consciousness about how a consensual marriage – and female pleasure – should function. 'Please G-d,' I prayed at the *mikveh*, 'help me come.'

I was seven months pregnant, for the third time, when I plucked up the courage to post: 'Does anyone else feel like sex is a duty?' People clamoured, concerned, to ask what I meant, so I posted the first metaphor for my sex life that came to mind: 'Well, if your child steps in dog shit you're going to clean it off their shoe, aren't you? You won't leave it. But you won't enjoy it.' I was encouraged by some users to move the chat to the website's hidden feature, where people can post in a safe thread that can't be found by Google. I was defensive of Zvi on there but I was also more honest than I'd ever been. 'It's not what you think,' I wrote. 'It's just that I'm gay.'

I'd never written those words down before but it was the simplest way to explain the dog-shit conundrum and hide the many other layers to what was going on at home. That first public admission unlocked something within me. I'd said it out loud now and I didn't want to stop. Later that day, I walked Talia around the crescent where we lived and repeated it to myself, out loud: 'I am gay. I am gay.' It felt incredible, like an unshackling.

The next day, I found Zvi smoking a cigarette in his usual place, on the step at the back of our house. It was August and I sat down next to him, looking across our little patio, unassuming in the evening light.

'I have to tell you something,' I said. 'I'm attracted to women and not to men. That's the reality for me and it's never going to change.'

'What about me?' he asked, inhaling cigarette smoke. 'Aren't you attracted to me?'

'I can't compare the two,' I explained. 'My feelings towards women and the obligation I feel to you, as my husband, are two different things.'

'Does it mean we'll get divorced?' he asked next.

'No,' I said. I truly believed I could do both: try to be loving towards him while acknowledging, but not acting on, this truth about myself. I didn't view this conversation as an ending so much as the beginning of a new, more truthful, leg of our marriage. He extinguished his cigarette, stood up and went inside, believing me as I told him things would carry on as normal. And they did.

Our third child, Roni, was born on 5 October 2012 in a hospital birthing pool. He had a bright shock of ginger hair that stood on end when we washed it.

I was discharged that afternoon and driven straight to the recuperation home. On that first day, as I breastfed, I entertained myself by scrolling between Mumsnet and Jewish blogs until one stopped me still in my tracks. A muckraking thread written by a frustrated Jewish activist had exploded with talk of a rabbi who was sexually abusing girls in London. The comments ran into their hundreds, full of angry, tired community members begging for internal change and at least a modicum of accountability. Buried among them, someone had written: 'What about Todros Grynhaus?'

Seeing his name knocked me sideways.

It was Friday night, moments before *shabbos*, and I went into the meal that had been made for the nursing mothers feeling that something was brewing.

Even against the discord of my life, I still loved *shabbos* and usually luxuriated in its calm washing over me. But this time I couldn't shake the thread from my mind, waiting impatiently for *shabbos* to end so I could go straight back on my phone. There were hundreds more comments waiting, with Todros's name coming up again and again alongside talk of girls he'd abused and cover-ups. Last time I'd told people his name, no one cared. Now, people were calling for him to be reported to the police. It awakened a determination inside me that I didn't know was still there. I was ready.

Back home, I scrolled the sites and chat rooms every time I fed the baby, eating late-night sandwiches that Zvi left for me on my bedside table, while I waited anxiously for more. I wanted a resolution.

It didn't take long to arrive. When Roni was three weeks old, Zvi took a call from my brother, Shmuel. Shmuel had been contacted by the uncle of another victim, who said that they were reporting Todros to the police and wanted to give my name, too. Zvi found me upstairs, sitting cross-legged on our bed, feeding the baby. I was used to men talking about me, making decisions about my life, but on this occasion I knew I had to take control. I told him I'd speak, but everything had to go directly through me. I didn't want my words distorted, passed from person to person like a playground game.

The next morning, I received a call from a female police officer. I agreed to give a statement and we set a date, in two weeks' time.

In the meantime, a rabbi got in touch who had given permission for the other girl to speak. He asked me two questions:

'Did he abuse you?'

'Yes,' I said.

'What would be your motivation in reporting him?'

'To protect other people,' I responded.

'OK,' he said. 'If you'd said "revenge", I'd have said no.' That wouldn't have fit his interpretation of the Torah.

The day before the officers visited, I went to Sainsbury's to buy two new mugs; the formality of a British authority entering my home was intimidating and I was fixated on the idea that I'd need to have enough mugs to make everyone a hot drink. The morning of the interview, I felt nervous but resolute. Two detectives, a man and a woman, arrived and set up a tripod in the corner of our dining room, nestled beside the bookcase containing a complete copy of the Talmud. Zvi took Talia and Noam upstairs and Roni slept in the buggy beside me while I spoke for five hours. I was worried I'd struggle to maintain my composure, but the moment I began talking I felt a familiar numbness wash over me. I checked out emotionally and told them everything.

10

The 149 bus

מִכֹּל עֵץ־הַגָּן אָכֹל תֹּאכֵל

וּמֵעֵץ הַדַּעַת טוֹב וָרָע לֹא תֹאכַל מִמֶּנּוּ

Of every tree of the garden you are free to eat; but as for the tree of knowledge, of good and bad, you must not eat of it.

Genesis 2:16–17

THE COURT CASE WOULD TAKE over two years to come to fruition. In the meantime, Noam was now five and sending him to a Charedi school was an important factor in keeping us on the path of belonging. But none of the ones near home that I'd hoped he would attend were prepared to take him, on account of me speaking up to authorities – something that had become notorious within our community.

One admissions secretary told me, 'You have to understand your son will not be accepted to a Jewish school.' I knew that wasn't the case and the arrogance with which she claimed to speak for an entire religion angered me. No matter how many doors were slammed in my own face, I wouldn't have my child ostracized. I hated the fissures that grew between those who were accepted and those who weren't; a community should solve its problems together. I noticed there were other parents without places, too, either because they weren't considered religious enough or because their kids had additional needs, so I made phone calls and collated a spreadsheet of thirty other families who were in the same boat. I took it to a local rabbi and asked for a meeting with governors from nearby Jewish schools, which he granted.

The meeting took place in his home, and when I walked through the door there were no more seats at the table. The governors were the only ones sitting down and the rest of us were crowding around, trying to get near. Unwilling to accept this power dynamic, I found a chair in the next room and pulled it in. All the governors were men in black frock coats and hats, and each in turn explained why theirs shouldn't be the school to take on any extra kids. Their interpretation of Jewish values repulsed me. I knew my religion's rules all too well and this exclusion, strategizing to protect one's own, wasn't in its spirit.

'Excluding children in this way is not how a community should operate,' I told the room, with some confidence.

The only remaining Jewish school that both had space and would take Noam was one back in Stamford Hill, so we made the difficult decision to return from the outskirts of London back to the crushing environment we'd been so happy to leave. Zvi's family were so thrilled that we were returning to a more Charedi neighbourhood that they sent us money to cover the higher rent, for a maisonette occupying the top two floors of a house there.

I may have lost my slightly less restrictive existence but I also gained the excitement of being in spitting distance of some cooler areas of London. Often, I'd walk Noam to school, take Talia to the nursery across the road, then get on the 149 bus with Roni and ride to the kooky little shops on Green Lanes and Stoke Newington High Street. I came from a place where everyone was formed in the same cookie-cutter image but these areas, where it was strange to be ordinary, felt inviting to me. It looked like you could be more than one thing all at once and the possibility of being part of it felt soothing to me. I let their cast of characters wash over me.

I would meander down the High Street, looking at ceramics, art and clothes I couldn't afford, or go to bookshops and flick through their lesbian sections and fiction shelves, reading books I was never going to pay for. I looked like a Charedi Jew but, among the hipsters and the punks and the multitude of people in their own national or religious dress, it felt like no one was assuming anything about me. Here, I was anonymous.

I'd had it drilled into me that Jews and non-Jews were meant to stay separate, yet here I was, crossing those boundaries and discovering, once again, that nothing bad happened. No fire rained from the sky. No chasms opened up before me. As I walked the streets, I educated myself, picking up social norms, saying hello to shop assistants as I ran my fingers along the sale racks hoping there was something I could afford, smiling at people I passed and listening in to what other mums and nannies spoke to each other about in playgrounds. In Stamford Hill, there was a strict hierarchy of who could greet who, but here, I made eye contact and enjoyed fleeting connections with strangers.

I was bridging two worlds and it made the discrepancies and hypocrisies of my own seem even greater. It also made me less reliant on Zvi for the social acceptability I had needed him for before. He wanted a rotation of dinner, TV and sex, but my own world was expanding and I was the one pushing at its walls.

With the court case pending and noise around it within the neighbourhood growing, I also felt able to talk more openly to people inside the community about what I saw as a cover-up of sexual abuse. I was less concerned about their judgement because I was receiving that anyway. I gained a bit of a reputation for being prepared to have difficult conversations and was invited to join a cohort of women who attended lectures in text-based Jewish learning together once a week.

The lessons took place in a classroom in north London and exposed me to the Talmud for the first time – which, as I had been told, makes a woman a prostitute. I was studying Torah, learning its Aramaic text and contemplating theological questions without any feelings of guilt. Not only was I invited to learn from female teachers who had studied and enjoyed their faith in a less restrictive space than mine, I was asked to write a presentation about what I'd learned and found great delight in presenting my new understanding of Jewish history to these women. I felt power and ownership, thrilled to finally feel included in my own religion. Best of all, I was surrounded by like-minded women.

One in particular, Eve, was the daughter-in-law of the former chief rabbi. Each week after the lesson, she would give me a lift to Brent Cross Tube station and we'd sit and talk in her Vauxhall Zafira. Eve and I were both from Glasgow but had vastly different childhoods. We were both women of faith but she was established in a professional world that I didn't know, though I was starting to want access to it: she was a tax accountant who had gone to mainstream school and university and had been lobbying for years against the lack of secular education for boys in Charedi communities. Eve was interested in the way I talked openly about what I was slowly discovering was a systemic problem that reached far beyond my own experiences and, together, we questioned what other systemic abuses were being hidden.

We egged each other on. I had first-hand experience of issues she cared deeply about. Both of us had fire in our bellies for fighting for others inside this world we were part of and that included a desire to lobby for change, no matter how uncomfortable that felt for everyone, including us. I had endured so much within the walls of my community, but it was my home. I wanted it to have the tools, the knowledge, to keep me safe and now, as a mother, to keep my children safe, so we could experience its best parts without fear of its worst. I was wringing it for the comfort I was sure it could give me.

Around this time, I had also started attending a support group for women who'd experienced sexual abuse. It took place inside a local library once a fortnight. There were half a dozen of us, and we were all religious Jews. When you speak that openly about such an awful shared experience, you get to know each other quickly and we became a sisterhood almost immediately. After sessions, we'd go for a meal in a late-night kosher restaurant and stay there, talking over plates of hot mushroom ravioli, until midnight.

Thanks to these groups that I found myself a part of, where we could discuss things that others didn't, little by little I was growing. In direct response, Zvi was folding into himself.

By the time Roni was fifteen months old, I was financially holding our family together. Zvi was barely working, while I had a new job that meant that I was vastly out-earning him.

My conversations at the support sessions meant I was also learning to say no to sex, which only added to Zvi's low mood. It didn't always mean that we stopped having sex but we had it less, quicker and I certainly stopped pretending to enjoy myself.

It was while I was sitting in the support group, around six months after I gave my police statement, that I next heard word of Todros. My phone flashed up with a number I didn't know. On the other end was a police officer. It had been weeks since I'd heard anything about the case and suddenly I was being told that Todros had been arrested and both he and his wife had been interviewed at a police station under caution. The officer explained that he had been released on bail, but just knowing that the case was progressing felt like an enormous relief to me. It didn't last. Within a week, I took another call. Todros had driven to Brussels, where he'd used someone else's passport – another man with a beard and Charedi clothes – to flee the country to Israel.

Months passed and every attempt by authorities to bring him back failed. There were points where this sense of powerlessness hurt so much that it left me catatonic, but every time, the women of the group would get me through, bringing meals to feed me and offering words of understanding to make me stronger. Then, one evening, while sitting at home, I got a call from another number I didn't recognize. An older lady spoke at the other end of the phone.

'My son's an airport chaplain,' she explained. 'He told me that Todros Grynhaus is on the passenger list for a flight arriving tomorrow morning.' The grapevine was working to full effect, and for the first time, in my favour.

I called the police station immediately to report what I'd heard. They confirmed that they already knew and had made plans to arrest him on arrival the following morning. He was taken straight into custody.

11

Here I am

הִנֵּנִי

Hineni. Here I am.

Genesis 22:1

I LOOKED DOWN AT THE oak frame of the witness box. The ends of my fingers were the only part of me that I could feel, my trimmed nails digging into the wood, rendering my knuckles white, almost grey. My legs couldn't hold me and every other part of my body was shaking. My palms were dripping with sweat. I thought I would slip and fall into a puddle of myself at any moment. That morning I had carefully painted on my make-up and brushed the creases from the pencil skirt, blouse and knitted cardigan I had picked out. I wanted to portray myself as powerful and put-together. There was no one downtrodden here.

It had felt impossible to step over the threshold into that grand space, like a theatre. Like a *shul.* I moved deliberately, picking up my right foot, then my left, and walking the three feet from the door to the witness box. It was a space that had been held open for me. For my voice to be heard.

I stood, motionless, in the stand. I could see a sea of twelve tiny faces swimming together. The jury. It reminded me of a page in my kids' *Where's Wally?* book. The women looked like ordinary people; I hoped the men were reasonable ones.

I looked down at the usher, then across at the judge, the lawyers, their wigs and gowns, ring-binder files and laptops. On my right-hand side a heavy red velvet curtain was drawn, to shield me from *him*, the man whose crimes had brought us all here. Everyone's eyes were fixed on me. I imagined his were too.

Someone below me cleared their throat. An usher, in a black cloak, was calling my name. I stopped looking around and tried to listen.

'Will you swear, Ms Fletcher, or will you affirm?' he asked.

'I will affirm, please,' I said, because the third commandment says you shall not take the name of the Lord your G-d in vain.

'I do solemnly, sincerely and truly declare and affirm that the evidence I shall give shall be the truth, the whole truth and nothing but the truth.'

My voice rang clear. I saw my voice in front of me, flying.

'A woman's voice is her nakedness.' I heard my mother's voice and pictured her pulling a tome from the bookshelf in our dining room, stabbing her finger at the codified rules around women's modesty.

Most of the people in the courtroom were men. But I didn't feel naked. Not at all.

'Ms Fletcher, please would you confirm your full name for the record?'

'Yehudis Gittel Fletcher,' I answered clearly. Loudly. I listened to the sound of my voice filling up the room. Everyone else was listening, too. The last time this case had been considered by a court, at the offices of the Beth Din, I was not even invited into the room. Now, my words were the reason all the men were here. I liked it. I was stating my name for the record because my name belonged there. *My* name. That was power. Not power *over* – I had no control over what the court was about to do or what the jury would decide – but power *in*. It was breath, oxygen. It was the beginning of my rise. *Hineni,* I thought. Here I am.

To my left, the judge sat at his bench. His grey hair was hidden under his wig. Like mine. He had an older face that I couldn't quite put an age to but it was more human and less distant than I expected, with the tiniest hint of a smile that crept up one side more than the other. He thanked me for coming, addressing me directly, his gaze meeting mine. I wasn't used to experiencing the male gaze on its own, devoid of lust or objectification. I realized that what he was looking at me with was respect. He spoke to me with respect, too. I was important and what I had to say, my contribution, was valued. And not just by him. The whole room needed me, to prove or disprove this case. I was so unused to it that it unmoored me.

My eyes fixed on the legal coat of arms that hung behind the judge: '*Dieu et mon droit*'. I looked it up later: French for '*G-d and my right.*' It reminded me immediately of the carving above the great wooden ark where the Torah scrolls were stored in my father's *shul*: '*G-d dwells before me, always*', inscribed in Hebrew. All those times I stood there as a child reading those words, reaching for them, wanting G-d, anyone, to listen. Now, at last, my pain was landing on listening ears.

The public gallery was full of men in dark trousers and white shirts there to support him, the strings of their prayer vests hanging out, as they swayed and prayed and tried to bring G-d into this imposing space too. What did *they* know? I was the one bringing G-d into this space.

The Crown's barrister was called Alistair and I just loved that: '*Alistair the barrister*.' Perfect. The lawyer for the defence was short and greasy, and in the years that followed I would spot his name in news reports, representing other people who tried to cover up the truth.

Their questions came in waves and I found quickly, easily, the ability to ride them with words until my mouth ran dry.

I listened intently. I held on to the barristers' questions and told the jury the truth. As I did so, my body language changed. I relaxed back into my skin.

I could not be, would not be, tripped up or confused by this room. I realized now that the people within it couldn't manage this thing without me. I wasn't the demure bride that the men I knew wanted me to be. I wasn't the administrator or secretary, translating for the religious men in the property office I worked in who couldn't speak English without me . . . Those people wanted me to be their facilitator or mediator, peripheral or replaceable. I wasn't. Not here.

I answered each question and waited for the next. At points,

I was brazen. I made my words heard, even the ones that repulsed me. *Erect penis. Seminal emission.* My words. My experience. My narrative.

'Isn't it true, Ms Fletcher, that you were not, in fact, so naive? That you knew exactly what my client was doing and that you participated in it?' his barrister asked.

'No, I was a child. I didn't consent to what he did and I didn't understand what he was doing.'

'But you were not naive, Ms Fletcher. Didn't you, in fact, wear trousers, baggy ones, with strings on the sides?' A little bit of vomit flooded my mouth. Who told him that? Who remembered me that way, a child with no hips and no breasts, wearing the super-baggy trousers that lots of girls my age wore?

At this point that very man leaned all the way to the edge of the defendant's box he was contained in and tried to catch my eye. Perhaps it was to intimidate me or control me or just see me. I didn't care which. He sickened me regardless. I turned away from his gaze.

Instead, I picked a woman on the front row of the jury bench and smiled at her. I was looking for connection, looking to answer the question about my clothes without losing myself in this man's game. 'I did wear trousers, the ones that everyone wore back then, with all the pockets and strings. Do you remember them?' I asked. She smiled back, nodding.

'Well, not everyone wore them.' He was struggling. 'No one else in your Charedi community wore them.'

I don't think the jurors cared about that.

He directed me to my video evidence, next.

'You say that my client asked you, "Where is your clit?"' His coarse handling of my memories blindsided me.

Now he asked me: 'You're a Charedi girl. How did you know where your clit was?' He over-pronounced the harsh 't', violating me again. I didn't want him to fluster me. I wanted to say the right thing.

The judge intervened. 'You don't need to answer,' he said. 'Ms Fletcher. You do not need to answer,' he repeated, looking straight at me.

I was so unused to being defended. Neither was I used to the collaboration or support of a man. I was not used to mattering in this way.

When I finally came off the stand for the first time, at lunch, I looked at my phone and saw a screen full of missed calls from Zvi. I called him back and listened to him tell me how hard what I was doing was for him. I was annoyed but tried to placate him for a while, until I didn't care enough to try any harder and ended the call. I didn't have the capacity to tend to his need for my attention.

When I stepped back on to the stand an hour later, I took a moment but no more to refind my stride. A large ring binder of plastic wallets had been placed in front of me, containing photocopies of evidence compiled and agreed upon by both sides of the case. The barristers talked me through its pages until we came to a photograph of a lock, attached to the bathroom door of the house where he had abused me. I thought about that house, a place I was supposed to live *in loco parentis*. I'd told the police during my interview that he used to jiggle the lock open from the outside and come in when I was in the shower.

'Ms Fletcher, can you tell me what you see in the photograph?' griped his barrister.

'I'm sorry, I can't actually see anything. It's really not a very clear photo,' I replied. I wasn't making this easy for him.

'Maybe I can help you,' he prodded again. 'This is the lock to the bathroom door at the home of the accused. You said that he opened the lock from the other side of the door, whilst you were in the shower. But he couldn't have – this is a photo of a slide bolt. You can't open a slide bolt from the other side of the door, can you?'

It wasn't the lock that had been there a decade ago and this was now so farcical that I was incredulous. I was grateful that I wasn't expected to mask or censor my thoughts here.

'He opened the door while I was in the shower,' I responded firmly. 'Do you not think people can change their locks in the space of ten years? Some people change their whole bathrooms more often than that.'

The jury laughed, in a measured way. He retreated but only briefly.

What followed was among the worst moments of the trial. He directed me to a note. I hadn't seen that note for a decade. It was written in pink highlighter pen on a sheet of paper from one of the thick supermarket pads of A4 paper that I used to do schoolwork on.

'*Tatte leibe*' – 'Dear father', in Yiddish. '*Please wake me up at 7 a.m.*' Then my sign-off, taken from that same inscription above the ark in my father's *shul*, written in perfect Hebrew: '*G-d dwells before me, always.*'

'This is evidence that you had thought of him fondly, is it not? That you wanted him to enter your bedroom?' His barrister was stooping and it filled me with a disgust and horror that sits with me to this day.

I had written that note as a child, aged fifteen, to the man entrusted with my care, entrusted to get me up for school each morning and to ensure I was home and safe each night. Why did he keep it? To wank over? As a 'just in case' defence stuffed in a drawer all these years?

The note was written in a mixture of English, Hebrew and Yiddish.

'Oh my goodness,' I said, making eye contact again with the woman who remembered the trousers with me earlier. 'Look at me, writing in three languages!' The whole jury connected, smiled. Sympathy, appreciation, humour – I don't know. I didn't intend for them to. The humour that had been mine since I was tiny came to the fore, and I was now so bold that I was peacocking. I'm sure it was disconcerting for the barrister. He had expected to be in the driving seat. But I wasn't the downtrodden girl he had hoped for.

By the time questioning came to a close, at around 4.45 p.m., there was no line of attack that I couldn't handle. After unleashing my new-found power, I certainly couldn't fold my voice back away inside me. I was taking that with me. There was no way I could return to a life of quiet dissent. But as I left the witness box, the adrenaline left with me. The trial had somehow managed to buoy me then leave me drained of everything.

On my way back home, I ran through the train station, into the public toilet, and vomited.

I didn't know what purpose my evidence would serve; whether he would be jailed for his crimes or not. I had no expectations. All I knew was that the experience had given me a new glimpse of what I was really capable of. As I returned to my children and my husband, I was sure now that I could do it all again. And I could do other things, too.

12

Hannah

וְנָתַתִּי לָכֶם לֵב חָדָשׁ וְרוּחַ חֲדָשָׁה אֶתֵּן בְּקִרְבְּכֶם וַהֲסִרֹתִי אֶת־לֵב הָאֶבֶן
מִבְּשַׂרְכֶם וְנָתַתִּי לָכֶם לֵב בָּשָׂר

And I will give you a new heart and put a new spirit into you: I will remove the heart of stone from your body and give you a heart of flesh.

Ezekiel 36:26

THE TRIAL PLACED A MONSTER in jail. Two and a half weeks after I gave evidence, the jury returned a guilty verdict. He was sentenced to thirteen years and two months behind bars for seven counts of sexual abuse against me and another girl.

The case became pivotal within the community, with the charge to take it to court led by a senior rabbi who had both brought it to the attention of authorities in the first place and testified for us, the victims, at trial. That it had gone to court at all and was receiving that kind of backing was highly unusual; the week after its conclusion, Britain's chief rabbi even went on record reflecting on the conviction and calling for further incidents of abuse to be reported to police without delay.

The question of reporting and, by extension, where schools should be doing more to support it, bubbled through the community, with senior rabbis breaking ground by publishing their positions on it, whichever side they fell on. These grubby problems were never usually aired in public. On the whole, there was a view that yes, we should be reporting incidents within the community to police but no, the authorities still did not belong within our schools.

The news had spread faster than even the grapevine could work. During the previous ten years, the rabbis had fought a losing battle against the sheer size and usage of the internet, and the sharing of big news like this online was now unavoidable. People I knew and those I didn't, those who'd heard the weeks of discussion or read about it in regional and Jewish newspapers, even the man who came to fix my washing machine, were approaching me, daily, through Facebook, on WhatsApp and in the street, to wish me well and thank me. They commended my bravery in speaking out and praised what I'd helped to achieve for the community.

But the people I wanted to hear approval from most, my parents and my siblings, gave nothing. My family did not see my actions as a service to the community; they were not proud of me. To them I had brought undue attention to our family and, to varying degrees, they were disapproving of the confidence that the case had stirred in me. I've no doubt that my brothers got harassed in *shul* because of it; I can imagine plenty of men funnelling their irritation, asking them to tell their sister to stop talking. Their dissatisfied reaction only sat at odds with that of everyone else I encountered.

Regardless of their opinion, the court case served a bigger, personal purpose. I was now a mother of three in my mid-twenties, and authorities outside of my community had taught me that I had legal status. My burgeoning sense of selfhood had ballooned and nothing could return to the way it had been.

I had a voice now. The trial had given me permission to speak louder than I ever had before, to stand up as a person and be counted on the record. And since my laps of the crescent chanting 'I am gay', I'd given myself permission to find out more about that part of myself, too. I was done with conforming.

I didn't know any other Charedi Jewish lesbians, but I had a childhood friend, Adina, from the synagogue school in Glasgow, who, in adulthood, had learned she was intersex. I'd seen her posting online about the freedom that being open about it gave her. It seemed to improve her life and I wanted to be able to evolve in a similar way. I messaged her on Facebook – a platform that, despite the internet's sinfulness, had become a necessary forum for discussing religion, just as it had for all other walks of life – and asked if she knew anyone else like us: people whose bodies or chromosomes or sexuality said a short, sharp, involuntary 'no' to the expectations of the deeply conservative society we lived within.

I enjoyed writing the words, telling her I was gay, without fear. There was already an acceptance among my closest friends and the women I had met through Torah study and victim support. They understood that I was married but attracted to girls, but it was never named. Being explicit about it was still new to me.

Adina was as keen as I was to find community so we launched a private group on Facebook called 'Queer folk in London from *frum* backgrounds'. Seven people joined. I was the only member who was married; most were divorced, one had fled the country to escape her wedding and another had come out as trans. All of us were insistent that it remain secret.

Among them was a woman named Hannah – the ex-wife of a rabbi and a mother to three children. Hannah had, with astonishing courage and some carefully managed scandal, come out as gay and been promptly ousted as rebetzen (rabbi's wife) of their synagogue. She was the only person in the group I didn't already know and was the first to suggest a real life meet-up: 'I would love to meet some like-minded people if anyone is interested.'

'I'm in,' I replied.

I set a time and a date for the following week, in a kosher health-food restaurant in Golders Green. Two others agreed to join us. I was sure that I would find a way to hold all the paradoxes of my life together, all at once, and making my first attempts at that both scared and excited me.

I walked up to the restaurant. It was 8 p.m. on a Wednesday in November; traffic was honking and the pavements were full of people wrapped up against the cold, spilling out of cafes and late-night supermarkets with their takeaways and shopping bags. I spotted Adina waiting at the door and, next to her, I recognized Hannah from her profile photo. Hannah was wearing a shirt and chinos – a butch little outfit – with dangly gold earrings and round glasses. Her chestnut-brown hair was cut short and she stood like a shy little boy, looking much younger than her thirty-two years.

I felt confident meeting these new people. I wasn't looking to recreate what I already had; rather, I was eager to make connections that felt more real than those I'd had in the past. I shook Hannah's hand and gave her a clap on the back. I was wearing a tube skirt, jumper, thick black tights and Doc Martens boots with a maroon wool fedora. I'd put the outfit together carefully to say what it needed to about me: I dress modestly and I'm gay.

We sat at a table for four and Hannah took the seat opposite me. On this occasion, I didn't have my wig on but instead wore the hat to cover my head, which is usual among *frum* women. Feeling more daring than ever, I scanned who was in the restaurant before deciding that it was safe to take off my hat, something I had never done before in public. Hannah was intrigued.

'If you can uncover your hair so easily, why do you cover it to begin with?' And so began an onslaught of questions.

'How can you talk so confidently about being a lesbian and yet go home to your husband tonight? Do you really think G-d wants the blessings on your food if you're sitting here with us?' she asked as our waffle stacks arrived.

Those things weren't contradictions to me. 'I can do it all,' I told her. I believed myself.

Hannah and I dominated the conversation. She explained to me what she'd been through, how she'd been thrown out of her home when she'd come out as being attracted only to women. I knew all too well that, for me, everything was at stake if I came out publicly, if my family knew. In my community, there wasn't a scenario where you could remain a part of our world as both those things: Charedi and a lesbian. They were mutually exclusive. But to me, Hannah represented an ideal. She was living a life that I wanted, a life in her true identity. She still lived inside the community, her children went to Jewish schools and she took them to *shul*, but she was open with everyone about her sexuality. Certainly, there were some places she wasn't welcome, but for the most part, she got to be all versions of herself. I wondered, for a moment, if I could do it too.

The four of us stayed there until gone 10.30 p.m. When I got home I checked on the children and heard Zvi asleep in our bed. Until hours ago I'd accepted this as my reality, but my mind was already preoccupied by the living testimony I'd just witnessed: there were more possibilities than this.

A couple of mornings later, a message appeared in my Facebook inbox, from Hannah.

'How are you doing?' And so begun a string of regular conversations. It always started with something simple like 'How's your day?' but quickly descended into more meaningful topics. We talked about gender or how we dressed or work or the kids. I didn't talk much about my marriage but I became fascinated by Hannah and her experience. I was also flattered and excited by a new friend wanting to know the real me better. My initial intrigue and relief at finding someone to relate to turned into a need to know her more. The Facebook group never met again in person but the connection between Hannah and me was only just beginning.

Our conversation over waffles had left me wanting to make another change. What Hannah had said about covering my hair stuck with me. I was astounded by my own ease in pulling off my hat in the restaurant that night. For years, I'd worn my real hair in a long braid that touched the bottom of my back when it was down, and which I tucked up under my wig or hat each time I left my house. Now, even if only for myself, I wanted to be able to see the real me when I looked in the mirror. I found a hairdresser in Stoke Newington who specialized in androgynous cuts and had them style it into a short, sharp bob, with an undercut shaved into the side. I adored it. Whenever I could afford to, I kept up my new style with visits to the salon, pulling my hair back under a snood or wide scarf or my wig each time I returned to Stamford Hill. For months, I told myself that there was beauty in this ritual of covering my hair, reciting my reasoning to myself over and over in my head – until I realized it no longer made sense to me. Who was I kidding? If I got rid of the wig, I was still the same person with the same faith. Surely, I was still a Jew?

I started wearing more hats – baker boys, beanies – which I wore with strands of my new hairstyle visible, the blunt edges of my bob on display. I didn't wear them in my neighbourhood but I'd wear them to Dalston and Brixton, where I looked no more out of place than every other hipster there. The change was less about an act of exposing my hair, as it was still largely covered, and more about the message I sent other people about who I really was.

At home, money was tight. Zvi was now so morose that his job was at risk and I knew that if he lost it we wouldn't be able to afford the rent. One day, approaching the joyful festival of Purim in March, Zvi came home from *shul* asking me for £20 for the charity collection that was traditional at that time of year. I had £60 to cover food and bills for the five of us for the rest of the month. We needed charity ourselves.

I was stripping the meat off turkey necks to feed the family and making the children pancakes for dinner three times a week. I dressed them up as a treat and counted out five chocolate chips for each of their plates to make the bag last for months. It was the poorest I'd ever been.

I was still saying no to sex, too, and one afternoon I received a text message from Zvi telling me to meet him at a rabbi's house when I'd finished work. He had told his father in New York about my refusal and my father-in-law had arranged for a rabbi to try to intervene, for the sake of his son's marriage. We spoke to him, this stranger, about our sex life, together, then separately.

'It's horrendous,' I told him. 'I don't want it – I'm not attracted to him.'

'I can give you a sedative to make it easier,' said the rabbi.

I listened in through the door as he spoke to Zvi. I heard the rabbi reassure him that no, he didn't need it as often as he thought or as urgently as he thought. In his mind, perhaps he thought he was trying to make peace between us, getting us to meet somewhere in the middle.

There was conversation but no resolution. At home, a couple of weeks later, I heard Zvi on a phone call at the end of which he beckoned me into the kitchen to talk.

'The rabbi wants to speak to you,' he said, offering the handset, set to loudspeaker.

'What could you cope with?' the rabbi asked me.

I thought for a moment. 'Maybe once a month,' I said. 'I could go to the *mikveh* once a month then have sex.'

'No,' said the rabbi. 'My starting point is twice a week.'

'I don't understand why we're negotiating here,' I told the rabbi. 'Where are you getting this from? Where does it say that I have to have sex with him?'

He started quoting various parts of the Torah.

'That's ridiculous,' I said. 'Which part of my body belongs to him?'

'Which part of his body belongs to you?' he came back with. 'You're the one holding him captive. You're married to him but you're not having sex with him.'

I told him I wasn't prepared to have the conversation and left the room. The issue needed handling for both of us, yes, but differently.

I relayed it to my brother Shmuel during a visit he made to London not long after, explaining how difficult and tense everything was.

'Zvi isn't working,' I confided, more concerned about the fragility of our household income. 'And I can't bear having sex with him.' The conversation was pragmatic, not emotional. It wasn't normal to talk with my older brother that way and I was embarrassed, but I was desperate. He obliged, though, and I was relieved that he was listening.

'He wants me to take pill packets back to back,' I explained. If I did that it would mean that I never had a period in between, so purity laws offered no reason that we couldn't have sex.

'You can't function that way,' he said, understanding my plight.

Then he asked: 'What's so bad about having sex?'

'I'm not attracted to him,' I said.

'You're not attracted to any men or just him?' Shmuel asked.

'I am not attracted to any men,' I said matter-of-factly. 'I'm not attracted to any *men*, including Zvi.'

'I know a doctor who can help you,' Shmuel offered.

No, thank you, I thought, but I took her name and number anyway. Matter dismissed.

I took his advice about the pills and stopped the packet. When my period arrived, it was my first reprieve from sex in months.

For Zvi, though, it was a religious reckoning.

One night, he said we needed to talk. 'I made a deal with Hashem,' he said quietly. 'I told Him that I don't believe that He would give me a wife who refuses to act as a wife should. If you won't, I don't think I can believe in Him.'

From this point forth, it felt as if Zvi outsourced his religious obligations to me. If I didn't come through – that is, perform my sexual duties – he wouldn't come through either: he wouldn't pray, observe *shabbos*, or restrict himself to kosher food. There was a kind of warped logic to this, a faith so simple that my individual autonomy could be prescribed to Him, and therefore taken as a sign of G-d's cruelty – giving Zvi something concrete to reject that wasn't me. At points, he'd flaunt his rejection of religion in front of people we knew, or check the calendar on his phone and tell me it had been thirty-nine days since we'd had sex. It felt like an attempt to embarrass me into submission but it served the opposite purpose: I stopped submitting almost entirely, giving in only occasionally when the expectation was so suffocating that, above all else, I wanted peace.

Shmuel had continued contemplating our financial situation and called a couple of weeks later to say he'd found a house in Manchester that we could rent. It would be much cheaper than London, alleviating some of the strain; I was exhausted from living hand to mouth. A move, to free up some of our income, felt like an obvious solution to at least one of my problems.

'I'm moving to Manchester,' I told Zvi over dinner that night, thinking not about my marriage but about survival.

'OK,' he said, passively. 'Let's pack.'

Noam was nine, Talia was six and Roni was four. It was now April 2017 and I'd made all the plans necessary to move our family across the country. Part of me hoped Zvi wouldn't come, but the other part couldn't imagine going it alone. I had outgrown him, yes, but I didn't know if I could manage by myself. All I could do was put one foot in front of the other again.

A few days before we left, I met with the support-group ladies for a final night, on the banks of the Thames. None of us had made huge life changes yet, we were all stuck in some way, but my decision to move was something at least, and, therefore, to be celebrated.

It was a clear spring evening and I'd had my hair freshly shaven underneath my bob earlier in the day. One of them wanted to see it so I took off my hat. She asked to put her hands through my hair, and each of our other three friends did the same, in turn. We stayed still, that way, for a moment, looking at the MI5 building across the river and illuminated

London behind it. I could feel a slight breeze coming off the water, against my neck, and I knew, when I went to Manchester, I didn't want to cover my hair back up.

We filled a removals van and drove it north, to the semi-detached house Shmuel had found for us with a big garden. It was inside the city's Jewish community but, a bit like when we lived in Edgware, it wasn't an entirely Charedi area of Manchester; that was just down the road. The rent was less than half of what we'd been paying for a hovel in Stamford Hill.

I hadn't lived in Manchester since I was a teenager being abused. I was pluckier now and I returned knowing that I'd made their streets safer by putting a paedophile behind bars. This time, I felt I was owed a welcome.

13

Thursdays at 6 p.m.

כִּי־קָרוֹב אֵלֶיךָ הַדָּבָר מְאֹד בְּפִיךָ וּבִלְבָבְךָ לַעֲשֹׂתוֹ

No, the thing is very close to you, in your mouth and in your heart, to observe it.

Deuteronomy 30:14

WORK HAD AGREED FOR ME to keep my job once I moved up north, paying for me to travel to London twice a week to be in the office. The rest of the time I'd work from a desk in a shared space in Manchester where no one else was Jewish. I saw that as an opportunity to dress 'gay'. I'd already uncovered my hair and this presented a chance to take my next step in matching my outside to my inside. I bought myself a cheap pair of skinny jeans and some men's shirts, which I began wearing, only on those days, with my Doc Martens. I put a long wool coat over the top and a hat, instead of my wig, to appear modest as I crossed in and out of my neighbourhood on my way to and from work. I took pleasure in the way dressing for myself made me feel.

We settled the kids in school and nursery and established a routine whereby Zvi would pick up, drop off and do the cooking, and I arranged everything else that they needed. The role reversal was a strain on both of us.

Hannah and I continued to talk, not continuously but picking up our chat when the busyness of life wasn't taking over. When time allowed us to speak, I was reminded of how much I enjoyed having her attention. Hannah often sent me photos with her messages but I was more shy. The first time I built up the courage to send a picture of myself was when I bought a blazer in the men's department of Primark and pinged her a mirror selfie.

'This is the first time I've bought anything tailored,' I typed. I was excited to see myself that way.

'U look really hot,' she said. This was new.

I replied, hesitantly calling her 'Babe'.

'Do u call everyone Babe?' she asked.

'Only a select few.'

I wasn't lusting after her but I enjoyed how it felt to be flirted with and found it easy to respond the same way.

By autumn, the following appeared in my inbox: 'Are things still complicated at home?'

'What do u mean by that?' I said.

'Are u not desperate to just escape and be free?' Hannah asked.

'I'm not willing to sacrifice the kids,' I replied, 'breaking up their family unit.'

'Ur deluding urself. Excuse the honesty but u are. Holding a marriage together for kids is crap.'

The idea of walking away from my marriage had never felt

like a real possibility. Everything I had been told growing up pointed to divorce as a failure that created broken homes and would damage my children. I didn't want to do that so I never entertained it. But the way Hannah now put it sounded more powerful than that and the fact that it was she who was offering it to me was incredibly attractive.

I replied in the most obvious way that came to mind: 'We should have a drink sometime. I am at Euston at 6 every Monday and Thursday.'

We set a date for the following week. I would be in Stamford Hill for work until 5 p.m. and always took the first off-peak train home to Manchester, at 7.03 p.m.

Hannah and I met at the front of the crowded train station. I felt excitement squeeze me from the inside as I realized there was someone waiting for me. I hadn't felt that before. I hugged her with my left arm and cupped her face with my right hand, only for a moment, while we kissed 'hello' on the cheek.

We sat down on the grass in the nearby square. I tipped my head forward, unclipped my *sheitel* and held it on my lap, shaking out my shaggy bob underneath. I enjoyed the look on her face as I did it.

Our conversation skirted around the edges; we talked about my job, our families, her university course. There was only an hour left until my train so we crossed the road and bought coffee in takeaway cups from a museum cafe. We warmed our hands on the cardboard coffee cups as we meandered back for my train, pausing on a bench outside the station while I waited for my platform to flicker on the vast departure board. In those disappearing moments, we got to the real conversation, the one we had been avoiding all along.

'Who is benefitting from you staying married, from living a lie?' she asked, calling out my bullshit.

It was true – I was living in an alternate reality that I'd constructed for myself: being a lesbian while married to a man; flipping my wig on and off as I pleased; seeing romance in maintaining half a life in order to fulfil the expectations of my faith. What Hannah said sparked a thought. Maybe this way of living meant my children were experiencing a repressed version of myself. That was no good for them or me. I placed my right hand on her cheek for a second time and said goodbye.

Our meetings happened almost weekly for the next nine months. It became a reprieve in my week that I looked forward to enormously. Sometimes we found a table at the pub next to the station or met in one of the many nearby cafes, but it was always just for an hour and we never touched beyond a hand on one another's face. We never discussed our growing feelings towards one another, which existed undeniably beneath the surface, and always saved the hardest conversation for last. As the weeks passed, the tension between us swelled. Each time, it became harder to say goodbye.

Darting between cities and missing the kids' bedtimes was also achingly hard. Spending *shabbos* together and taking them to the children's services at synagogue was a highlight of my week. I loved sharing the most joyful parts of my faith with my children, and *shabbos* with them felt like calming, happy days that were to be cherished. Days that enveloped them and me together. *Shabbos* was the day that I felt I could mother at my best, because the world around us stopped.

Each week, I would find moments to pray alone at synagogue, too, blocking out the sound of the gossiping women and the rabbi's sermon that echoed around my ears to speak to G-d privately under my breath. 'Please G-d, help me cope,' I'd plead. Sometimes I'd cry, hiding my face with my prayer book, as I looked for G-d's comfort. Just like when I was a child, I didn't always get it but it didn't stop me asking. The difference was that these moments weren't miserable to me any more. I welcomed them, I wanted them. They felt like a little bubble of love, a holy little space, that I created for myself and for G-d.

We had some more money again, by virtue of the move north, and were mixing among a more modern Jewish crowd, who still dressed and behaved modestly but in a far less conservative or traditional way than those in Stamford Hill. The women wore more form-fitting, trendy clothes that still covered their elbows and knees, and the men wore *cappels* (skullcaps) with secular outfits – jeans and shirts. Their households were traditional but existed more in the modern world, while still keeping the pillars of their faith.

As a family, we found ourselves on a circuit of *shabbos* lunch invitations and I could see that the other couples we shared meals with were intrigued by me. I had more in common with the men, who also travelled for work while someone else was at home making dinner, and this anomaly, in an otherwise traditional world, made me interesting.

I was savvy, too – a negotiator – and I was doing well at work while also deftly handling our affairs at home. I got used to this life where we had enough and things just about worked, but every now and again Hannah's words jumped to the front of my mind and I'd return to the idea with Zvi, broaching whether being together was what we really still wanted.

He'd threaten that if we split, he'd get custody of the children and I'd have to pay him maintenance. I was free to leave, he'd say, but because he had been unemployed for years and had therefore done all the school runs while I worked and travelled, the children would have to stay with him. We performed the same argument like actors in a play, always reaching the same conclusion. I may have been strong enough to reject his advances in the face of manipulation and godly ultimatums but I still believed he held the upper hand in our home. The one thing I couldn't do was abandon my children and he knew that – I breathed to the rhythm of the rise and fall of their own little chests; their flesh was mine. I couldn't leave.

In June the following year, when the children were ten, seven and five, we were at my brother Elchanan's house in London. Elchanan noticed what friends in Manchester had already seen: that Zvi wasn't following the rules of our faith. My brother was surprised by his small infractions, like showering on the morning of *shabbos* or skipping prayer services. Within days, phone calls began bouncing back and forth among relatives, fretting about our religious status. Both our fathers were talking to each other, and each, in turn, was making calls to the Beth Din. Meanwhile Zvi was telling all of the other men now involved in my marital and household affairs that I wouldn't have sex with him, in order to rationalize his disobedience. My father-in-law called me a *moredes*, a fallen woman who doesn't abide by her wedding contract. A grave insult.

On my side of the family, Leah decided it best that we call a meeting between her, Mummy and Daddy, who were in London on one of their visits from Israel. We all sat together in her dining room, which had been extended in the years since my two engagements had taken place there. It is unusual for matters of marriage to get to the stage of sex talk among kin at the dining room table but on the odd occasion that they do, it's open season. Everyone – including plenty who weren't sat in that room – had taken a view.

Leah opened the conversation: 'Men can't just walk up to women they see and have sex with them,' she warned, reminding me of my responsibility to satisfy my husband's urges. 'You have to be there waiting for them when they come home.'

My father didn't like this: 'What do you think men are – animals?' he said, standing up for his gender, for himself and, unwittingly, for me. I was surprised by how it felt to have him on my side.

Then my mother intervened. 'Men can't survive without sex,' she said sagely. 'No wonder he has no job, feels the way he does and doesn't want to observe – you won't have sex with him.'

After all that I'd endured in two marriages, it was my husband's non-observance that had finally got my family worried. To be married to someone who was irreligious would damage not only my reputation but the whole family's. G-d knows there had already been enough of that, and it was of grave concern to them.

My father put the conversation to bed. 'If you're not having sex and he's not religious, you should get divorced,' he decided. Then he added, 'You shouldn't be having sex with anyone you don't want to.' I still feel sure that this opinion came from him wanting men to look more noble than I was experiencing them to be but, nonetheless, hearing those words come out of his mouth made me feel that, this once, my father was protecting me.

This was my exodus.

I was completely afraid of how this would all work: the moving out, custody, how I'd survive, but at least they were keen to help me get the ball rolling. Practicalities came first; the divorce would follow. My salary still went into mine and Zvi's joint account. There had never been a discussion about who that money belonged to - it certainly didn't feel like it was mine to touch. While I had a bank card for the account, I didn't have the passwords to move money around or take it out, so I had no means of putting down a deposit on a new place. However, when a tax rebate landed on my doorstep a few days later, containing a cheque for £212, a friend took me straight to the building society, where I was set up as a vulnerable customer. 'We're here to help you,' the clerk said. Thank G-d.

On a Tuesday night after putting the kids to bed, I went downstairs to Zvi, who was sitting in the armchair watching TV. I took my usual spot on the sofa and turned it off.

'I want to talk to you about something important I've been thinking about,' I started. 'I don't think we should stay together.'

He looked up. 'You beat me to it by a week,' he said, resigned to our fate, then switched the TV back on.

I called work to ask for six weeks off while I sorted out our new lives, which included finding a job for Zvi, who also needed to pay for his own place. Work refused.

'You're either here or you're not,' my boss said. So, I left.

They put my final month's salary in my new account and I applied for benefits.

My brother Shmuel arranged for me to live at Grandma G's mews house, which he managed for my father. It had been rented out since she'd died, a few years earlier. Now, as if G-d had intervened personally on my behalf, their tenant had left in a hurry and they needed a new one. The children and I would move in, paying market rent – no mates' rates for me – and on 27 August 2018, the day before my thirty-first birthday, that's what we did. My parents helped me move and took me to buy towels and dishes, all with the familiar undertone of 'Yehudis Gittel, what have you done *this* time?' When I kissed the kids goodnight, turned off the lights in their bedrooms then climbed into a bed of my own, I experienced pure joy. I'd achieved the impossible and there was a world stretched out in front of me that I could finally touch.

14

Accidental activist

כִּי֩ אָנֹכִ֨י יָדַ֜עְתִּי אֶת־הַמַּחֲשָׁבֹ֗ת אֲשֶׁ֧ר אָנֹכִ֛י חֹשֵׁ֥ב עֲלֵיכֶ֖ם נְאֻם־יְהֹוָ֑ה מַחְשְׁב֤וֹת
שָׁלוֹם֙ וְלֹ֣א לְרָעָ֔ה לָתֵ֥ת לָכֶ֖ם אַחֲרִ֥ית וְתִקְוָֽה

For I am mindful of the plans I have made concerning you – declares G-d – plans for your welfare, not for disaster, to give you a hopeful future.

Jeremiah 29:11

Though Zvi and I were separated, I was keen to make the divorce official and be free of his name. In Jewish law, a woman cannot divorce her husband; it's her husband's right to divorce *her*. Powerful men could, however, step in to speed up the process on my behalf, and, as a rabbi, my father was in a much more esteemed position than my soon-to-be ex-husband. Zvi's irreligiosity meant that my father was keen for me to be disassociated as swiftly as possible with this man. He made some calls and had my religious divorce – the *get* – arranged within a fortnight. I didn't feel that this intervention, on my father's part, was ever about my well-being – it was clearly about my Judaism – but I was grateful that he'd done something for me nonetheless. It felt like love.

A presiding judge called me on my mobile before the ritual divorce hearing that would happen in front of the Beth Din. He had heard, from my father, the terrible news. 'Tell me,' he said, querying what had led Zvi astray, as he carried out his diligence. 'Was it because of the internet?' I left him to believe that it was.

A few days later, I returned to that same building in Manchester where I'd left my evidence when I was sixteen. It instantly took me back to being a teenager and I was filled with the same trepidation. I was ushered into a side room to speak to the judge – not an actual legal judge, a rabbi. A friend came with me for support. The halls were dingy and cold and the judiciary offices were behind a wooden door with a keypad lock on. Inside, the rooms were almost bare, with perfunctory plastic and chipboard furniture.

For a *get* to be granted, the paperwork must contain every name you've ever been called, in order to be wholly accurate. An officer and I established that this meant my divorce was to be ascribed to Yehudis, Yehudis Gittel, Gittel, Judith and Gertrude.

Zvi dashed into the building long after I got there, his hair still wet from the shower and dripping on to his shirt, and my friend and I were sent into another room to wait while he spoke with the rabbi for hours.

When the rabbi decided it was time, Zvi and I were invited into a large office with scratchy navy carpet, where three rabbis and two witnesses sat behind a long table. I was surprised to clock one of the witnesses take out his lunchbox and start eating his sandwiches as proceedings began.

Zvi and I were asked to walk to the front of the room to perform the ritual that dissolves any Jewish marriage, as set out in the Talmud for every couple, regardless of how religious they are. Zvi looked nervous. He was told to first drop the handwritten divorce paper, with all our many names on it, into my hands. I was then to tuck it into my sleeve, walk to the door and come back again. I didn't once meet his eyes.

With a mouthful of lunch, the sandwich-eating witness asked us to redo all of this twice for certainty – this wasn't customary, just annoying.

Zvi then recited the inverse of the words that he had said under our *chuppah* during our marriage ceremony – '*Harei at muteres le'chol adam*': 'Behold, you are permitted to all men.'

Not without my say-so, I thought to myself.

And with that, I was free.

I was thirty-one and a single mother, sharing custody with my children's father. I walked out of those doors and embarked upon adjusting my outside again, this time to look more like my inside. I went home and put my remaining modest clothes to the back of the wardrobe, replacing them all with T-shirts, jeans and jumpers. My hair was already uncovered by this point but now I exposed my skin to the sun for the first time, too, and I treasured every freckle that formed on my shoulders and forearms, like little kisses from G-d.

I messaged Hannah.

'Hannah,' I wrote.

'Hi how r u?' she replied.

'I'm single, that's how I am,' I texted back. 'Feels like I've been born again.'

Grandma G's mews house was right at the heart of the community and I now looked nothing like the people who lived, shopped and worked around me. Twice divorced, uncovered and dressed in jeans, people distanced themselves from me. Parents at the school gates who would have said hello previously now averted their gaze. Others I knew from *shul* crossed the road when they saw me. But after years of hoping to fit in with these people, a new inner confidence was emerging that meant I didn't need their approval. Outwardly my conformance had changed but my inner faith was as strong as ever. My new persona felt increasingly natural to me, even if it was something that others struggled to get their heads around. I still went to *shul*, because I loved it, just as I did when I was a little girl. I wore a suitable skirt, respectful that I was in G-d's house, but my head remained uncovered as I was no longer married. After the service, people made conversation with each other but no longer with me. I talked to the kids instead. The lunch invitations dried up, too.

Nonetheless I said all the same prayers I'd always recited in my head as I went about my daily life, making blessings when I ate, washed or started something new, and so on, and my children continued at the Jewish school, where I valued them learning about their heritage and being able to hold their place within their own community. None of this had ever been about leaving Judaism behind.

Zvi and I also obtained a civil divorce, which came through a few months later. There were no assets to split and it was handled, simply, by solicitors and by post – all perfectly unceremonial. My friend Shevy, who lived round the corner, added me to a single mums' WhatsApp group called 'Superwomen'. There were around two dozen of us – not an insignificant number in our community, where divorce was far rarer than the mainstream. We organized our own *shabbos* lunches to replace those we'd attended in couples, potluck and child-centric, at one another's homes. Our get-togethers were a haven away from the rejection and judgement we had all experienced for leaving our marriages. We were perceived as a threat to other women's husbands and a bad influence on the women themselves by demonstrating that we could manage on our own. I was so happy to have back some camaraderie, and to celebrate *shabbos* with other people like me.

I had no doubt about what I wanted to do next. I wanted to see Hannah. The inescapable reality was that through all our 6 p.m. meetings, the Facebook chats and the text messages we continued to send back and forth, I was beginning to fall in love with her.

In October, for the last of the High Holidays, the kids and I went to stay with Elchanan in London. I conformed in their observant household and did things the way they would expect. They were aware of my divorce, but I had hidden almost everything else from them. I never lied to them but I chose carefully what I shared. I was terrified that they might find out I was a lesbian. I knew there was no way they would accept me. Hiding was tiring but, in return, they were supportive of my new circumstances, which is what I needed.

On the final day of the holidays, I arranged to meet Hannah for prayers at an alternative synagogue, where women were allowed to actively participate. I thought it sounded incredible and I was desperate to go. Finally, I could take an active role in my own faith. It was three miles from Elchanan's home and the same rules applied to holy days as to *shabbos*, meaning no one could drive me, and the walk would be too long for my two youngest. Undeterred, I borrowed a double buggy, stacked them in seats one on top of the other and set off, with Noam holding my hand alongside. I had loaded the buggy with snacks and we walked for two hours across north London.

Eventually I trundled through the gates of the *shul* and saw Hannah waiting outside to meet me. She smelled good, like musky men's fragrance – Creed, I later learned – and was wearing a leather jacket that looked incredibly sexy on her. I sorted out the kids and we walked into the synagogue and took our seats together. Someone gave each of the children a packet of crisps and Hannah sat beside them, chatting to them as they munched away, making them smile, melding with my family. Everything felt right. It was a new way of worshipping and it suited me.

Hannah was among the people who had prepared a portion of the Torah to read from that day. I watched as she got up and walked over to the *bimah* – the platform in the centre, usually reserved for the rabbi to lead his service – and read aloud to the one-hundred-plus women who had gathered to be part of the service. As she read, in fluent Hebrew, she met and held my gaze. I'd never been so turned on.

Yes, I thought. I was definitely ready to love a woman.

I waited until the day's end, when I could use technology

again, and switched my phone back on. I messaged Hannah: 'I can't stop thinking about you.'

'Stop thinking about me,' she wrote. 'Forget about me. Go to sleep.'

She told me I was straight out of a marriage and that it was too soon for me to go down that road. I was upset to be pushed back, but so used to people dictating my life that it didn't shock me.

I tried to sleep but the next morning there was a new message waiting. Hannah was driving over to see me so we could talk about it. The children were happily playing with their cousins when she arrived, so I slipped out of Elchanan's front door and walked around the corner to where Hannah had parked up, out of sight, in her white Nissan Micra. I climbed into the passenger seat and asked to hold her hand. We hadn't done that before.

She placed her hand in mine, smaller than my own, and our fingers interlaced. I felt like I'd found what I was looking for.

She told me all of her fears about entering a relationship with me: that I was fresh out of my marriage and hadn't been with anyone else, that she didn't want to be my rebound and didn't want a long-distance relationship, either. To Hannah, these details felt impossible to overcome but I saw them as circumstances that we could navigate together. I had spent so long unshackling myself that I didn't want to waste any more time. We were operating on stolen moments and didn't have the luxury of time to reach a conclusion. I needed to get back before my brother and his family noticed that I wasn't in the house, so we left our discussion unresolved, but it struck me that, for the first time, I was looking at a future for myself in which I didn't compromise who I was – a Charedi lesbian in love. From then on, all I could think about was Hannah.

In Manchester, Zvi and I had agreed that the children would spend three days a week with him, and four with me. I was living on benefits and thin air but I was finally able to make financial decisions about my own money. Without the burden of supporting Zvi too, I could budget effectively and that made life easier. Grandma G's house wasn't beautiful – it had a grubby white facade and the first thing you saw was a roll-down garage door – but we had enough space for all of us. The two boys shared a room and Talia and I each had our own. I could still smell my grandmother's scent in the walls and I cherished it. I slept in the bedroom that had been my mother's until she married my father and I had a little study downstairs where I filled the shelves with books that I'd chosen, not that I'd been prescribed. Pages full of feminist theory, political autobiographies and Jewish commentaries, which had been forbidden to me when someone else was in control, were suddenly mine for the choosing.

Buoyed by my new-found independence, I bought myself driving lessons. I was determined to learn how to drive and award myself even more freedom. My instructor, Paul, was a part-time caretaker at the children's school. He was a 6ft 4 skinhead, sixty years old and an ex-policeman. Paul treated me like a person, an equal, and his respect and confidence in me helped me to pass my test within a couple of months. I had inherited my grandma's ancient Toyota Yaris, which Zvi had driven when we were together, and suddenly I could do anything. It opened up the world to me.

With more time since quitting my job, I ramped up the lobbying that had been a constant hum of ambition for fellow activist Eve and me since our women-only lectures in north London. In the months since, I had been stepping outside my immediate Charedi community to build alliances, first within senior Jewish leadership, then, gradually, outside it, with charities and people involved at grassroots levels, in shaping social policy. I had been speaking to all of them about sexual abuse and systemic cover-ups within the community, which I was now beginning to see extended to other types of abuse and restrictions on rights and civil liberties. Children, I'd come to realize, were particularly vulnerable through their lack of education, and I had first-hand knowledge of how that left them in the line of danger.

My passion for advocacy really took off when a friend alerted me to a severe physical assault that had taken place in a Charedi school in London. These schools cater to Charedi boys from the age of three and are modelled on little *shtetle* schools that their proprietors imagine their ancestors attended, in pre-Holocaust Eastern Europe. Inside, they teach, almost exclusively, Jewish studies in a mixture of Yiddish and Hebrew. The pointed lack of English serves parents eager to isolate their children completely from what they see as negative outside influences, including the usual school curriculum. They are attended by the most conservative of Charedi families, and their archaic approach to teaching is also, unfortunately, reflected in corporal punishments handed out to pupils deemed in need of discipline.

My friend had come to me in the hope I could intervene, because I knew how to navigate the world and authorities outside the community. I knew who could help and, more importantly, I was unafraid of having difficult conversations. She knew the potential fallout should she raise her head above the parapet, but I was already ostracized so that was no longer my concern. I used a whistle-blower button on the UK government's website to raise the alarm and was surprised by the speed at which I received an email asking if I'd be willing to attend a series of meetings about the bigger problem. I was keen to have the ear of authorities who I believed could help my community and I accepted, alongside Eve. The meetings grew in size each time, escalating to larger groups, with attendees from more and more government departments, who were all keen to gain an insight into keeping children safe, beyond just this case. Speaking up with purpose came easily to me. In fact, it was harder now to stay quiet. It felt like a responsibility.

Not everyone nearby felt the same, of course. One morning I opened the front door to take the children to school to find a pile of dog shit had been left on my doorstep. I shuffled the kids back inside, grabbed a scrubbing brush and rubber gloves, shut the door behind me and cleaned it up.

Woah, I thought to myself as I piled the kids into the car. *That's a lot of effort to invest in pissing me off.* I was disgusted, but rather than instilling fear, it just made me more defiant. If this was the worst they could do, it only served to spur me on.

Eve and I formalized our advocacy work and began taking payment for our efforts, establishing a fledgling think-tank with a small group of allies, called Nahamu, meaning 'be comforted' in Hebrew. It was our call for people to come together, acknowledge harms within our community and hold each other as we changed and grew together. The changes we were pushing for would not come from Jewish leadership, we knew that. But maybe they could come from us, with help from the outside world.

I wasn't even six months divorced and it had already been a whirlwind. At the end of the year, I reached out to Hannah again. We had barely spoken since our conversation in her car, but our feelings, our longing, had not gone away; they had simply been put on pause. The thought of us, of a possible life together, never left my mind. I messaged to say that I was coming to London for the bar mitzvah of a friend's son, and she invited me to stay at hers. Although confused by the mixed signals, I felt a thrill when I read her message, and agreed. When the day came, I stayed at the party long enough to be polite before taking a taxi to Hannah's, where I arrived still in my modest shift dress, arms covered, out of respect for the celebration I'd attended, but my lips painted deep red, which was not so modest.

I put my bag down by the front door and greeted her in the same way we always had at Euston: my right hand on her cheek. I followed her to the living room, where we sat at opposite ends of the couch. I wasn't quite sure what I was doing there but it felt good to have someone to go home to.

Hannah's kids were at their father's, so it was just the two of us and we spoke for a while before she broached the question that loomed over us. Did I want to sleep in a spare room or with her? I answered in a split second: 'If I'm sleeping here, I want to sleep in your bed.'

Her bedroom was small, little bigger than a box room, and furniture was limited to a low double bed pushed against one wall and a broken dresser with clothes spilling from its drawers. Deep fitted cupboards disguised a boiler hidden inside a recess in the wall. The sight of the laundry piled on the floor relaxed me; I didn't have to impress Hannah – no one here was going to judge me.

I stripped down to my vest and boxers and waited for Hannah to use the bathroom before I did. I returned and climbed under the sheets, not knowing how much space to take up or leave between us. Downstairs, we had been clear to one another that whatever feelings were charging through the air, we would not have sex that night. But the bedroom was crackling.

Just as I had been the first time I stepped into that all-female club in Soho, I found myself terrified of what I was feeling as we lay facing one another – of how much I wanted to touch Hannah, and for Hannah to touch me. I was embarrassed by the ferocity of what I felt, a heat that I'd been taught forever to push down, and I didn't know how to read her.

We tossed and turned, talking for hours, gradually moving closer to one another, until we were almost nose to nose, trying to ignore the building tension. In the dead of night, Hannah took my face in both her hands and kissed me.

15

All those who are forced to choose

קְרָא אֵלַי וְאֶעֱנֶךָּ וְאַגִּידָה לְךָ גְּדֹלוֹת וּבְצֻרוֹת לֹא יְדַעְתָּם

Call to Me, and I will answer you, and I will tell you wondrous things, secrets you have not known.

Jeremiah 33:3

FOR THE FIRST TIME, I was with someone by choice. I felt wanted by Hannah and it took me less than two months to say 'I love you'.

Every two to three weeks, we travelled between Manchester and London to spend the weekend together and forged our own, new routines. We hosted *shabbos* meals for friends, sharing the grocery shopping, prep and the cooking, getting dressed together for *shul* that evening, then coming home to set out the food, dress salads and serve our guests' drinks like a well-oiled machine. We took all the Jewish bits we loved and made them gay. In doing so, we filled our tables with people who were either conforming and longed not to or, like us, had stopped conforming and wanted to sit at a table where they were simply accepted and could also relish in the traditions they were raised with.

I began an education too. I knew very few women who'd been to university. In fact, I had been taught that they were forbidden spaces for us.

'Universities used to be much cleaner – they're filthy now,' my mother would use as a blanket dismissal when I queried what happened there. The irony was, of course, that she herself had studied English at one before marrying and becoming so religious.

But ever since Todros had pulled me out of school and sent me to work in the print house, I had longed to study again. With no formal qualifications and only a matter of weeks until the new semester started, I emailed the admissions tutor for the University of Salford's Social Policy course, told them my story and explained how I wanted to understand more, to make sure that my activism came from a place of knowledge and not just reactive experience. One meeting later, I was sent an unconditional offer to study. I was over the moon.

Being in an educational establishment of that size, with its warren of study rooms, lecture theatres and libraries, was brand new to me. So was the way in which the vastness of what I was learning nourished me. I was hungry for it all. My father agreed to reduce my rent by £300 so that, with care, I could just about afford student life, and I was grateful for this meaningful help from him. Studying took up a lot of my time so, when Hannah and I weren't able to meet, we'd arrange video dates in the evening where we'd sit on the sofa, each with a cup of tea, and catch up. Sometimes, my doorbell would ring and it would be a delivery driver with a box of chocolates Hannah had ordered from the Co-op.

'How much do you love me?' I'd ask when I called to say thank you.

'To the Co-op and back,' she'd reply.

When we were together, I felt more like myself than ever but each time we had sex, my past hung over me like a thunder cloud. The pleasure I craved from being with her was dampened by the fact that, despite never feeling this safe in bed with someone, I couldn't feel my own skin. It would take months of being together before I could have an orgasm.

In public, when Hannah tried to take my hand, I would pull back, afraid. I worried that being out would impact my charity work. I didn't want it to distract from the task at hand and, more than anything, I was constantly afraid of what my family would say and do when they found out.

Hannah and I couldn't hide for ever, though, and the reality was that we didn't want to. I lived in a neighbourhood where everyone breathed down one another's necks and, as if that weren't claustrophobic enough, I was inhabiting a tightly packed mews where households took note every time a door opened or closed. So, when Hannah came to stay, neighbours and familiar local faces inevitably saw us together. I learned to handle their curiosity by meeting their gaze in the park where we walked on *shabbos* afternoons and wishing them a prompt 'Good *shabbos*', or by being the first to say hello when we passed them doing our grocery shop. It was all very cordial on the face of it, although I also discovered that the street had established two WhatsApp groups as a response to having lesbians in their midst: one with Yehudis on it and one without Yehudis.

Holding back in public was becoming futile. But despite that, I really wasn't ready for my parents to find out about us. I knew the time would come when I'd have to confront them and hope for their acceptance, but in the meantime, I tested how it felt to be out, in a lesbian couple, in more and more places – first the shopping centre, then the deli and the coffee shop on the kosher high street, knowing that in doing so I was edging ever closer to that time. With my parents in Israel, word was bound to reach them but I'd delay it for as long as I could.

I was lying by omission. Whenever I did speak to my family and they asked who I was spending time with, I told them it was a friend. If they asked what I'd done at the weekend, I'd tell them about the walk or the meal but I wouldn't say I'd stayed over with my partner. It was almost as dishonest as lying outright and it made me just as uncomfortable as it did when I lied to my mother about washing my hands as a child.

When autumn brought Rosh Hashanah and the High Holidays back around, I rang the *shul* office to book seats for the services, as congregants were required to do for the busiest days each year.

'I have a new partner,' I told the secretary. 'I need an extra seat please.'

She was excited for me and asked where, downstairs, he wanted to sit.

'She's upstairs, with me,' I replied.

'Please hold,' came the answer. After several minutes of the loudest kind of silence, she allocated us seats F9 and F10 in the ladies' gallery and said goodbye.

Hannah and I weren't touchy-feely in *shul* but we stood out. All the other women were dressed the same way, in heels and florals and hats and wigs, and we both looked like a polished version of something else, something super-gay, in buttoned-down shirts and chinos. I had long since determined that the rules around how I should dress were man-made rather than divinely inspired, and now, with Hannah by my side, I abandoned the need to wear a skirt even in G-d's house. We were all naked before Him anyhow, weren't we? It would have been so easy not to go, not to put ourselves or others in the awkward path of other people's judgement. I was sure now that they must be reporting back to my family, although my parents hadn't said anything. Ignorance was bliss for the time being. This was my *shul*, my faith, my holiday, too, and I had no intention of letting go. I loved it. People greeted us as though it was exciting to have someone different in their midst. Plenty of them wouldn't have wanted us involved any further in their lives but we were gossip-worthy enough to feed their dinner conversations and they were happy to keep up appearances by not being rude to us in public. I could just imagine them, though, telling relatives about the butch lesbian couple at *shul*. Our social status among Manchester's local Jewry was progressing some way towards being notorious.

The flip side of putting my sexuality out in the open was that people no longer knew what to do with me, like the rabbi who used to stop and ask how I was but was now awkward and cold. Then there were those who cared both about

Jewish law and about me as a person but didn't want to – or didn't know how to – choose between the two. Some had us round for *shabbos* lunch, some never spoke to me again. I was an anomaly for which there was no protocol in our community, so their reactions were always unpredictable, and often disheartening.

In early 2020, Hannah and I were invited to a bas mitzvah in London: it was our first party invitation together. I felt nervous again – all our firsts made me nervous – but I assured myself that no one there knew my parents or my immediate community; these were more secular Jews, who didn't cross over with other parts of my life, so I hoped we could just enjoy it as a couple in love. There was a DJ and a dance floor where we danced to songs I hadn't heard before. I'd heard some secular music by now – Destiny's Child and Katy Perry featured on a playlist I'd made myself – but my exposure only scratched the surface. A couple of weeks after the party, the host – a friend of mine – sent through pictures of Hannah and I that had been taken on the night. The only pictures I'd seen of us together before that were ones we'd taken of ourselves on our phones, snapshots of intimate moments in the car, at the park or at home. This was the first time I'd seen what someone else saw when they looked at us. I found it hard to believe that it was me beaming back. Though my inner confidence was still growing, my ease in who I was becoming was already visible from the outside.

When we were invited to attend Eve's son's bar mitzvah a couple of months later, I still couldn't shake the fear that with each outing, the day I'd have to face my parents' judgement was creeping closer. Nor could I stifle the pride I felt in going to another celebration as one half of my couple, but these two feelings rubbed along more uncomfortably with each passing day.

Before the party, Eve explained to me that her son's Torah portion – the passage which he would recite in front of their guests – contained the line in Leviticus that amounted to orthodox Judaism's condemnation of being gay: *You shall not lie with a man as you do with a woman; it is an abomination.* Eve had become a true friend and I had grown close to her family, so I was touched when she called about this. She and her son asked me to write something to share as part of the ceremony, to read out before this verse and hopefully offset the hurt it could cause to those who were gathered, to anyone like me. In consultation with Hannah, I came up with a blessing and in Eve's north London garden, I stood in the marquee that had been put up for the prayer service and felt my voice shake as I delivered what I'd written:

> He who blessed our fathers, Abraham, Isaac, Jacob and our mothers, Sarah, Rebecca, Rachel and Leah, may He bless all those who suffered as a result of the verse we are about to read. All those who bear their sexuality and gender identity as a yoke around their neck. All those who are excluded and are unable to live their truth. All those who are forced to choose between the love of their families, and acceptance from their communities, and loving as they were created. Let us say 'amen'.

I heard the words leaving my mouth and found it difficult to accept that it was my voice I could hear. That it was me who, not yet a year after a divorce, after starting my independent life, had the opportunity to say these things, on behalf of others, in public. It caught me off-guard, even as I spoke. When I finished, I stayed at the front until the portion of the Torah that was being read was complete. It gave me about three minutes, all of which I needed for my heart to slow down, my face to stop feeling hot and my legs to regain the strength for me to walk back to where Hannah was sitting.

I sat down and she squeezed my hand. Women in the rows in front and behind us turned to me and whispered '*Shkoach!*' 'Well done!' A couple of them stretched out their hands for a handshake. When the prayers ended and guests mingled in front of the buffet table, even more sought me out to thank me for my contribution.

Those moments of visibility were becoming more common in my day-to-day and they served to instil confidence that helped me to grow in endeavours elsewhere. Before I knew it, I had a brimming schedule of advocacy, charity work and study. I was appearing in the mainstream press, and on TV and radio, too, as a talking head for what I was fighting for. All this alongside raising the kids and finding time for my relationship with Hannah. It was my ability to live my truth that fuelled me.

In May, the *Jewish News* named me number six in a list of forty people under forty to watch in the community. Hannah proudly announced this on her family WhatsApp group. She had come out to her family years earlier and had already been through that process with them. Hannah's family faced negativity and judgement from others for giving us even the most rudimentary acknowledgement and acceptance as a couple. Hannah's mother had to face the double threat that not only was her daughter out and attracting attention, but she was also with me, who now had a public reputation of my own. But they were, to varying degrees, kind and supportive of our relationship, more so than I feared mine would be. Hannah had the freedom to share our life with them and deal with the nonsense that they came up with in response to it. I couldn't help but feel disappointment and envy that I wasn't in a position to do the same.

In all the public discussions that had arisen through my advocacy, I had continued to keep my sexuality hidden. I was convinced that, if I shared it, that would be what people would focus on and it would distract from the campaigning work, which was what mattered. And then there was the small matter of my parents finding out. I still had to address this issue, but watching Hannah discuss my achievements with her own family made me start to imagine that it could be more possible than I had previously thought.

The next few months weren't straightforward for Hannah and me. It wasn't just that we lived in different cities and weren't able to see each other, but we were both single mothers with little time to ourselves. After the divorce, mine and Zvi's shared custody arrangement had worked for a time but, by now, it was strained. He had let me know he was struggling to keep up with caring for them and the kids were spending most of their time at mine. Hannah and I spoke constantly and tried to keep up our online dates to provide respite at the end of tiring days.

I had started work one day a week as an independent sexual violence adviser (an ISVA), supporting victims of domestic violence and sexual abuse who had reported it to authorities.

I worked with women in my community, helping both them and the police to bridge the gap between the two worlds and the rights they frequently didn't know they had. It was time-consuming and hard. It often left me emotionally depleted but it was important work.

That June, Hannah came up to Manchester with her youngest child, the same age as Noam, to spend a week with us. We'd never parented together and I was apprehensive, but despite its challenges, facing the minutiae of daily life together propelled our relationship to the next level. More than just enjoying having someone I loved to sit and talk with and hold at night, we began to see, with greater clarity than our snatched weekends offered, how it might look if we lived together, and we spoke, properly, about doing so more permanently. How many bedrooms would we need, we wondered. How would we manage our children? Or deal with differences in the way we parented or the way that we loved and needed love? Where would we live? We began having more serious conversations about the future, but finding ourselves on the precipice of change, again, brought trepidation as well as excitement. I found that as much as we could talk through our obstacles when we were together, sitting on the same sofa, living in the same house, in the same city, each time Hannah returned to London and we were apart again, communication became more difficult, more snatched, more tense. Our ability to navigate life as a twosome was slipping and, at points, I found myself feeling like we were operating within entirely different dimensions, particularly when it came to parenting.

In July we had a huge blowout over the phone. I'd had a

difficult few days worrying about custody arrangements with Zvi that had quickly escalated and were more complicated than ever. He was erratic and not coping well with life, let alone parenting. He didn't communicate with me to any effect, which made it hard to keep things consistent for the children. It was time-consuming and distressing but the people that mattered most to me, the kids, were my sole focus. Hannah was dealing with her own stresses at home and, when we came together on the phone to try to discuss it all, neither of us gave the other the response they were looking for – or maybe, the response we each needed. We didn't speak for a week.

It was Hannah who broke the silence, with a text.

'I'm so angry with you,' she wrote. She was worried about how my custody issues were going, too, but mostly, she said, she was angry.

'It's OK to be angry with me,' I replied.

I was reluctant to discuss the ins and outs of my situation when we hadn't spoken all week but I knew we needed to talk. And we did – we made time for a video call that night but resolved nothing. She wanted space but I needed to fix a time when it could be guaranteed we would pick up the conversation properly. In the days that had passed since we'd last been together in person, I'd gone from picturing our future together to worrying whether it would ever happen or could even work. The not knowing was too agonizing to face without an end date.

'I need a time frame,' I said.

'Three months,' Hannah told me. And with less emotion than I thought, that was it: we stopped speaking and focused on our families. It wasn't easy – I thought about her every day – but I had been through enough to know how to compartmentalize and make the most of whatever head space I'd been given.

Two months later I messaged her. It was my thirty-third birthday.

'Babe, would it be possible to talk earlier than we said?' I asked.

She agreed.

'We need to talk properly and hold each other,' I wrote.

'So, so much,' said Hannah.

A couple of days later, I took the train to London. My train was due in at 11.36 a.m. and Hannah came to meet me at Euston, at our usual spot on the square outside. Again, I placed my hand on her cheek. She'd booked a room in a cheap hotel nearby where we could stay for the night and have the privacy we needed. We hailed a black cab from the taxi rank outside Euston and said little during the ten-minute journey through town. The hotel felt deserted. We checked in at the reception desk and took the lift up to the small, functional room. I took off my coat and sat on the end of the bed. There was something urgent between us. The need for touch, I thought. We part-undressed, then held each other, my arms wrapped around all of her. The past few months had been so intense; so much had happened. Hannah could see it in my eyes. She paused.

'Did you come to London to dump me?' she asked.

'I wouldn't phrase it that way,' I said.

Silence.

'But we need to not be together.'

The weeks apart had given me space to realize that this was not the right time for me to be in a relationship. Maybe she had been right all along, ever since that night outside Elchanan's house, sitting in her car, when she'd warned it was too soon for me. I also told Hannah something I hadn't told anyone, something I'd feared since I'd first said the words 'I'm gay' out loud. Was the reason that I wasn't attracted to men because I'd been abused? If I tried dating other men, was there a possibility that I could find myself attracted to one of them? These thoughts had resurfaced during our break, and I felt compelled to find out.

Hannah was visibly shocked by all of it. I understood why. I could see how much I was hurting her and I felt terrible inflicting that pain on this person I'd chosen, who'd chosen me, too. Two hours passed and we held each other as we cried. We didn't stay the night; it would only have prolonged the pain. We took a cab back to the station and, with a hand on one another's cheek, we said goodbye.

16

Put away your begging bowl

יְהוָה לִי לֹא אִירָא מַה־יַּעֲשֶׂה לִי אָדָם

The Lord is on my side, I have no fear; what can man do to me?

Psalms 118:6

Between my marriage to Zvi and my relationship with Hannah, I'd been single for all but a minute and a half.

I met a friend for a coffee on my local high street, in Manchester, a stretch of road in the early stages of its gentrification, bookended by the non-glamour of two supermarkets, with coffee shops springing up in between, in the spaces once occupied by charity shops. We sat down at a table in one of the cafes and started talking about dating. I told her what I'd been wondering to myself and what I'd told Hannah. Could I date a man? Had the issue just been that I hadn't had a relationship with one I felt safe with before?

She asked me: 'If you were to date a man you actually fancied, what would he look like?'

I pondered for a moment. For the life of me I couldn't

imagine one that I found physically attractive. She clocked my confused expression as I tried to grapple with the task she'd set.

'OK,' she said. 'Ignore his face. That might be off-putting. What about the body? What part of his body might you find attractive?'

I thought and thought. 'Maybe his forearm?' I offered. It was as much as I could muster.

She laughed. 'You're a lost cause.'

She was probably right, but I wasn't quite done with the experiment. I wanted to be absolutely sure. I was already on a Facebook group for divorced Jewish people, not for dating but one where men and women talked about custody schedules or what it's like to be on your own for the High Holidays. I dipped in now and again and, occasionally, I posted in my usual shoot-from-the-hip, slightly sarcastic tone. After one such post, a man in New Jersey dropped into my inbox, asking if he could get to know me.

He had already read my entire Facebook page and, I presumed, googled me, as he seemed to know an awful lot about me before we even got started. I found that a bit weird but he lived in the USA so it seemed safe enough to talk some more, given that he wasn't likely to turn up on my doorstep.

He was quite a bit older than me. He said he was heavily involved with his kids, which I liked, and they stayed with him half the time. From his profile, he didn't have an ugly face, either, and seemed reasonably intelligent. There was enough that interested me in our conversations that made me think it was worth sticking it out. After some weeks of back-and-forth, we arranged a video call, which seemed a normal next step when you're considering quasi-dating someone on the other side of the ocean.

His face appeared on screen. He was handsome, with a square jaw and ready smile, but within three seconds my only dominant thought was *nope*. Definitely nope. I was still not in any way attracted to men. I didn't want to be rude so I chatted for a while. I even took part in the dating game he'd prepared, like an awkward 'get to know you' icebreaker at summer camp. Plain or spicy crisps? Early riser or night owl? Biden or Trump? I stayed for long enough to seem reasonable, before cutting the call short with some lame excuse. Now, the experiment was done.

Of course, my thoughts instantly returned to Hannah. Communication with her hadn't ended when we left each other at Euston station. We were both hurting but remained on friendly terms, checking in with each other frequently. We were both single parents trying to exist in a community that didn't know how to keep us and we needed one another's support in this world. On top of that, in truth, the love between us was far from extinguished.

When October came around and I went to stay with Elchanan for *Succos*, the harvest festival at the end of the High Holidays, I arranged to come off the motorway a junction early to see Hannah. She answered the front door and we kissed hello on the cheeks. The kids were with me and Hannah put on oven chips and chicken schnitzels for their lunch while we caught up. Being together again in the same room felt like a dance as we navigated new emotional territory, but the talking came easy. I didn't realize how much I missed the familiarity of being in her company. Or the electricity that still fizzed between us.

A couple of days later I asked my sister-in-law if I could leave the kids with her while I went out to see a friend for the evening.

'Go out, have a nice time,' she said. Elchanan and his wife were always just a bit more facilitating of my new life than the others were, although they still didn't know that I was a lesbian. I felt bad keeping the whole truth from them but that's what I needed to do, just for a little longer.

Hannah picked me up, down the road, in the Micra. She had packed a picnic supper for us – more schnitzel and chips – which we took to the Welsh Harp, a reservoir named after the old pub that used to stand on its banks in Hendon. We sat on a short wooden jetty that poked out over the water. It was 10 o'clock and pitch black, cool but not freezing, and we were wrapped in coats and scarves. We sat facing each other. Gradually, as we talked, I realized that my whole body had leaned into hers. She put her arms right around me and we kissed. We went back to Hannah's and had the kind of sex that, for the first time in my life, allowed me to feel every nerve ending in my body. I lay with her until 1.30 a.m. then went back to my brother's house feeling unlike I ever had before.

That hot sex, hotter than when we were first together, continued whenever the opportunity allowed, and we decided, for now, we were best off just enjoying a physical relationship. It felt good that way. It was uncomplicated.

When the kids broke up for the winter holidays a few weeks

later, Hannah and her youngest child came to stay with us for the full two weeks and we functioned like any other family. We were meant to be just hanging out, figuring things out as we went along, but it was only a few days in that it became clear how easy life felt together.

'I've been thinking,' Hannah said one night on the sofa. 'I should move here, to Manchester. With you.'

I agreed. And I was so excited. But we had to do it carefully, we were sure of that much. The reality was that neither of us really knew how to do this thing we were doing. We'd both had therapy, separately, after leaving our marriages and we certainly hadn't come from simple backgrounds. I hadn't been in a relationship by choice before Hannah, and that was part of what had made it difficult to relax into it the first time around. I didn't know how to be vulnerable with anyone.

We decided we'd benefit from embarking on therapy together to figure out how we could blend our families. Doing so felt like a necessary hand-holding experience for me, to graduate to the next stage. It gave me the space to learn, too, because neither of us, we agreed, had the skills to learn on our own and our failed first attempt had proven that to us.

We held our therapy sessions over Zoom every two weeks. Where possible, we were in the same place, sitting together at a kitchen table or on a sofa, but sometimes we had to do it from our living rooms in different cities. One of the clearest things to come out of the first few sessions was how big a factor my fears around my family's reaction were in terms of how we moved forward. I had been so determined that when I came out to them it would be for me and not for anyone else, even Hannah, but in holding back from telling them I wasn't allowing us to take our next steps. I was freezing us in time. Besides all of that, I had to reconcile with the fact that it was a fantasy for me to even consider that they still might not know about us after our *shul* outings, my public profile and the community chatter near home. My whole family, me included, had been operating on a 'don't ask, don't tell' basis, so we didn't have to confront the reality. The truth was I was afraid: afraid of their rejection and afraid of their abandonment. I was afraid of disappointing them.

Four or five sessions into therapy, our therapist made an observation that ambushed me.

'You go around begging for stuff that people aren't willing to give you,' she told me.

She helped me to see that I came from a place of such a low expectation of love that I begged for others, including Hannah, to see me as a person entitled to it. I wanted so badly to be loved that I had spent my whole life so far folding myself into a version that was acceptable to other people, even if it wasn't acceptable to myself, just so I could feel able to ask for morsels.

'Put away your begging bowl,' she instructed.

I don't know if I gave what she said more meaning than she intended, but those five words resonated intensely. *I am not a beggar*, I thought. So, I stopped: I stopped asking for permission and acceptance; I stopped prostrating myself and making myself into what others might consider likeable, loveable. In my working life, I knew the value of listening to everyone else's needs, now I had to learn how to state what I myself needed. I wanted to wean myself off being the fixer, the helper, the always-available friend, the Yehudis who drove to London, cooked, filled my sister's freezer with food when she had twins then drove back home. That wasn't the kind of connection with others that I needed to pursue any more. As a mother, I had to try to untangle myself from my children's daily roller coaster of emotions and, as a lover, I had to work hard to stop my insecurities skewing my new relationship any longer and really open myself to receiving the love I was being offered. In reality, that meant a shitload of arguments as we negotiated what we each needed but it felt like productive work, clearing the decks before we made our plans for our future. It deepened our connection and it unlocked my next level of freedom as a result.

Meanwhile, in my activism work, Nahamu was ready to fly. If women needed to leave their husbands, or were being harassed by their exes, or discriminated against at work, they came to me. Sometimes their mothers or fathers did, too, seeking advice from someone who understood both worlds – my world. Eve and I had produced our first paper, with an aim to influence national policy, and it focused on a topic that came up again and again when we explored the systemic abuses within our community: forced marriage. As we'd drilled down on the issue of children's safety, we'd spoken to so many Charedi parents who had reflected on their own experiences of getting married and their experiences of marrying off their children. They all tipped to the same endpoint – that for anyone to do anything, to graduate into adulthood in any way, within our community, they had to get married. Each person we spoke to described the impact of practices that we all knew and recognized and celebrated:

engagements that took place after young people had spent only half an hour together, that were agreed to by teenagers who would have to have sex on their wedding night but had received no sex education. For some, this process began at sixteen, routinely at eighteen.

Of course, my own experience existed in the background, but this was much bigger than just me. Using what I was studying at university, I looked at the existing legislative framework on forced marriage and overlaid it with these practices from my world. I saw that when this happened to other young people in other walks of life, there was a name for it and a statutory process to deal with it. It was defined by law and acknowledged as a crime. But when it happened to us, no one noticed.

Eve and I had discussed this in meetings with advocates and local councils in areas with large Charedi communities, with government departments and with Jewish leadership groups. We told all of them what we had found. We spoke to organizations tackling forced marriage in other communities, too, even people who had been involved in writing the original legislation. They all reinforced that what we were hearing and describing was, of course, no different from what they had also campaigned against. This legitimized what I was assembling. I could not only be confident in presenting my findings but know that they were dearly needed beyond even the community that I was a part of.

As I discussed the matter more and more in the run-up to the paper's publication, people within the community remained sceptical that we could change anything. The reality was there was no longer room for them to remain in denial about its problems. But they were scared about how we as a community would be perceived when this came out. And there was pessimism and low expectation from those within more mainstream, liberal Judaism, who were inclined to dismiss what I was putting forward as 'just what religious people did'.

By the time we were ready to publish, in February 2021, I was confident that what we had put together was groundbreaking, not just in Britain but in Charedi communities globally. I knew that when we came to approach journalists to try to get some coverage, it would be an easy sell. And it was. We made headlines internationally.

I was profiled in *The Times*, where I told my own story in more depth than I had before, and interviewed on Radio 4's *Woman's Hour* and by the *Telegraph*. On Yiddish-speaking chat boards, and in Jewish forums, it was everywhere. And everyone had something to say about it. Some people thought my actions were horrendous and claimed it was anti-Semitic of me, a Jew, to call out our community's faults; others recognized that while they might not like how it was phrased, there was no disagreeing with what I was saying. As I told a *Telegraph* reporter: 'We don't have time for anti-Semitism to be eradicated before we address harms being perpetrated within our community. Bigots are responsible for their own bigotry. We have work to do and no time to waste.'

It elevated my status as an advocate and it was an enormous boost to my confidence. It felt like a demonstration of a power and ability that had been within me all along and, most importantly, I was seeing the impact of what I'd done in real time. People were messaging in their droves and commenting on forums to thank me or share their own stories. They would tell me that my work encouraged them to break the cycle of forced marriage within their own families. I received a letter from the government minister for safeguarding, thanking me, and the prime minister even responded to journalists' questions raised by the publication of our paper.

The message that touched me most was from a father in his sixties who reached out on Twitter as he and his son waited to board a flight from London to New York, where they were meeting his son's potential bride. He said that because he'd read about me and my paper, he made a point of telling his son over and over again that if, at any time, he decided this wasn't what he wanted, they could turn around and go home.

For my family, I sensed that the publication was another 'Yehudis Gittel, what have you been and gone and done?' moment. I'd sent my father the draft some weeks earlier and told him that it was going to be in the public domain soon. He'd told me that he was upset that I'd been critical of *halachic* practices (those dictated by Jewish law). He didn't agree with the detail but he had at least engaged with me on it and, for a moment, I felt like I was a 'jolly good fellow' in his eyes. That made me feel good. I don't think he had anticipated the impact it was about to have, however. Even I couldn't have anticipated that.

After my paper exploded, the family adopted the same 'don't ask, don't tell' approach to dealing with my advocacy work as they had with my very obvious lesbian relationship. I hoped that, within their response, there was an element of being impressed by me – impressed by the fact that the world was listening to their daughter and sister. It didn't, however, distract from the fact that they fundamentally disagreed with what I was saying and did not remotely welcome the attention that my notoriety was bringing to our family name within both the immediate and wider communities. Nonetheless, I'd sometimes spot my mother and father occupying a screen tile in the audience of webinars I was speaking on – just silently observing, I presumed, or perhaps keeping track of me.

Both during public-speaking engagements and in conversation with those that surrounded me, it was often suggested, or even presumed by some, that I should leave, or that I had left, my community. Many wondered how I could remain, given the changes I'd made to my own life and the changes I was calling for more widely. The possibility of leaving my Judaism behind had always been there and, in a way, it would have been the most obvious option. It was all I'd ever seen and it was all that was depicted to the wider world, especially with shows like Deborah Feldman's memoir *Unorthodox* taking off on Netflix. It's all that the people who jumped to those conclusions knew, whether they were in or outside my community: you were either in or out; you either looked and behaved how a Charedi adult was expected to look and behave or you didn't. There was no grey area. But the words of a teacher in one of my classes stuck with me: 'I'm not threatening to leave,' she had taught us. 'I'm threatening to stay.' How perfect.

It was harder for everyone, including me, to fight this battle and make changes to myself and my world from the inside, but I already had roots and I already had an identity, founded in my faith, that enriched me, that I loved and practised. Choosing to stay as a lesbian who questioned the rules – when leaving would be so much easier – made my choice all the more important, because it created new options for others, too. I protested against anyone who suggested I was no longer part of this community because of my decision. Without realizing, my very existence had become my resistance. Once I recognized that, I became more insistent about staying and more comfortable with the idea that living as a lesbian wasn't sinful or something to be ashamed of. I was providing an example for anyone who wondered whether it was possible to be Charedi like this, in my generation or the next. Staying in the community as a lesbian became, for me, a holy thing to do.

17

The bar mitzvah

בְּהִתְעַטֵּף עָלַי רוּחִי וְאַתָּה יָדַעְתָּ נְתִיבָתִי בְּאֹרַח־זוּ אֲהַלֵּךְ טָמְנוּ פַח לִי

When my spirit fails within me, you know my course; they have laid a trap in the path I walk.

Psalms 142:4

We were planning in earnest for Hannah's move to Manchester. Once we moved in together, I knew there could be no more pretending with my family and I was OK with that. It was time.

But there was one more thing I wanted to enjoy before I spoke to them and risked the consequences of saying what had gone unsaid for so long. Noam's bar mitzvah was in May. The lead-up was busy and complicated. Zvi and I were still trying to figure out co-parenting. We had to navigate this celebration together, though. Bar mitzvahs are when, in Jewish law, a boy, aged thirteen, becomes a man and reads in synagogue for the first time, celebrating with the people who love him. It was usual for bar mitzvahs to have hundreds of people present but this would be a small affair with a few dozen friends, family and congregants invited across a weekend of celebrations. I wanted it to be perfect for Noam.

I had to come to a decision with Hannah about whether she should be there to celebrate Noam with my family. We both agreed that she shouldn't. I'd waited this long, and putting them all in a room together for the first time, now, would deflect attention away from him. It was the right decision, but we felt sad about it nonetheless.

For the Thursday-morning service at *shul*, when Noam would be called to read from the Torah, there would be small celebratory breakfast boxes for guests to enjoy after wishing him *mazel tov*. Then, on *shabbos* morning, when he would read before a slightly larger congregation, there would be a *kiddush* – food to nibble, cake, and wine to toast the bar mitzvah boy – and a bit of personal branding – an N for Noam and the date – on serviettes and the like for decoration.

'I'll arrange what you need for the *kiddush*,' Shmuel, the brother who lived nearest, offered, which was kind.

I was grateful for his help and the financial support. I had very limited money, living on a student loan with bills coming out of my ears, and my father had said he would pay for Noam's bar mitzvah lessons but didn't, so I'd already spent more than I could afford on tutoring in the past year.

I thought we might forgo the customary Friday-night dinner but Shmuel was insistent we should have one with some of the family. A dinner to honour the bar mitzvah boy, in a function room or, for those more flush, a marquee, was quite usual, but it was expensive. Shmuel said that the meal was part of the bar mitzvah expectation, part of the rite of passage, so he would host it for us at his home around the corner in Manchester.

'It's big enough, there's space,' he said. His pious wife, Rachel, who was tall and broad with a bouffant blonde wig, agreed to split the cooking with me. Again, I was thankful. I'd spent so long managing a family on my own, it was a relief to share the load at such a pivotal time.

I had planned on my parents being there but, in the end, they didn't fly over from Israel; they said the travel arrangements would be too complicated for them. My sisters had travelled up for the Thursday morning before returning to London and I had spent the week buying and cooking food. When I arrived at Shmuel's to assemble it all with Rachel on the Friday morning, I was surprised, given their kind offer, to be handed receipts for both the food Rachel had bought and the *kiddush* catering that Shmuel had said he'd take care of. Had I misunderstood his offer? Perhaps he'd only meant to help with the organization of the party, rather than the funding of it? I put the bills in my pocket and resolved not to think about them until after the weekend.

When Friday night came, my three brothers, their families and mine gathered at Shmuel's. My sisters didn't stay; with almost two dozen children between them, they said, it was too hard for their large families to come. I bit my tongue, though I knew full well that for any other event they would have managed just fine.

Shmuel's house was flash, brimming with gaudy decor and chandeliers. The dining room had leather sofas at one end, a bookshelf crammed with holy books at the other and an enormous mahogany dining table in between. One wall was adorned with an embossed metal tableau of biblical Jerusalem, flanked by framed portraits of rabbis. *Shabbos* candles in silver holders were ready to be lit as it turned dark. It was warm outside, but the room felt chilly to me; the yellow light from the chandeliers felt too bright.

To be the mother of a bar mitzvah boy is *a thing*, let me tell you. I should have been a queen that night but I felt like hired staff brought in to cater and organize my own *simcha*, the word we used for a happy occasion. I spent the entire evening scurrying around, hosting a party that I'd been strong-armed into throwing and now with no idea how I was going to pay for it. As the meal went on, more and more of our cousins poured in to wish Shmuel – not Noam or me – *mazel tov*.

On *shabbos* morning, we arrived at synagogue to watch Noam read again. This was the biggest moment in the bar mitzvah weekend. Noam still had the stature of a little boy. He wore a navy-blue check suit and new, shiny, black brogues. Even Roni had a little suit to wear and Talia a floral dress with a leather jacket. We walked in and the *shul* felt huge.

I looked around and wondered if we were there too early. The seats were far emptier than I'd expected. My brothers were seated downstairs but most of the other relatives I'd invited – cousins and sisters-in-law, nieces and nephews – had stayed home without excuse or explanation. I took my place in the women's gallery and looked down to watch my son, looking like a tiny man in his new suit, peering over the scroll laid out before him on a platform in the centre of *shul*. I'd sacrificed Hannah's presence for my family's but they had deserted me, deserted Noam. I looked to either side of me and soaked in the fact that it was my friends, not my family, who were there to share in my pride. It both devastated me and made me determined: determined to get on with living my life, out and proud, once the bar mitzvah was over.

As if to hammer home their point, two weeks later my niece, Dov Ber's daughter, got married. I attended one of her *sheva brochas*, the nightly parties that take place during the week after a wedding. Shmuel was hosting at his house again and I imagined he would put on something similar for our niece to what he'd done for Noam's bar mitzvah dinner. I got there, however, to find the whole house full of people. My parents had flown over, Shmuel and Rachel had hired furniture covers, the tables had floral centrepieces and each was set with expensive wines and custom-made chocolate miniatures for the guests. The contrast between how they celebrated her and how they celebrated my child was painfully apparent.

Already upset, two things happened in the following days that left me with a creeping sense of uncertainty. The first was a conversation between my mother and me. I tried to make small talk by commenting on the gold bracelet that she was wearing, one of four family heirlooms inherited from my Grandma G, and intended, eventually, for each of my three sisters and me. I admired it against my mother's pale skin and told her offhandedly that it was my favourite out of the four. She didn't look up. She simply unpicked the clasp and clamped it on my wrist there and then, urging me: 'Have it now.' Her eyes showed kindness and yet this act felt foreboding. Did she know that something was about to change? Did I?

The second was a conversation with pious Rachel, who had told me a few times during the course of the wedding party that she needed to talk to me when it was all over. A couple of days later she sent me a text with a priced and itemized list of the lemonades that had been drunk from her larder at Noam's dinner and the groceries – avocados to be precise – that she'd bought that same morning for last-minute catering. This was on top of the bills she'd already given me. Rachel asked me to come over to sort it all out and I did so, arriving at theirs on Tuesday morning.

I walked into the kitchen and she exploded at me: 'You make me so angry I can barely tolerate being in your presence!'

I had a feeling this was about more than lemonade.

'If I make you so angry, why did you offer to host the bar mitzvah?' I asked.

'It was very difficult for me,' Rachel replied. 'But it was the right thing to do.'

She spoke *at* me for an hour. She said she needed to tell me how she felt, how she couldn't bear to watch me go around talking about what I'd experienced, and what she thought of me for doing so. I let her talk until I couldn't any longer.

'Hang on,' I said. But Rachel couldn't hang on. She couldn't control how she spoke to me, she said, and I could either take it or not.

I decided not, thank you, and stood up to leave. But before I did, I pulled out a short stack of £10 and £20 notes that I had withdrawn to pay my debts to them, the money I owed them but could not afford. I threw it at her, walked out of their front door, and got into my little grey Yaris, which was parked up on the street outside.

I looked out of the windscreen and up at the sky. It was June and there was a drizzling mist coming down from Manchester's summer clouds. The tensions in our family had been growing quietly high for too long, a hierarchy of affection that left me, Noam, Talia and Roni on the bottom rung and meals and meetings dampened by awkwardly inconsequential conversations in which nothing was said, or at least not when I was in the room. It couldn't go on. I started the engine and began driving to Shmuel's office. I knew what I needed to do next.

18

Rejection

כִּֽי־אָבִ֣י וְאִמִּ֣י עֲזָב֑וּנִי וַֽיהוָ֣ה יַאַסְפֵֽנִי

Though my father and mother abandon me, the Lord will take me in.

Psalms 27:10

THERE WAS NO DOOR ON Shmuel's office. Maybe he'd got the idea from a management manual or maybe he'd just never got round to putting one in. He'd recently bought – but not committed the time or money to converting – the flat above a former bank and used it to house his little property empire. It stood among the convenience stores, charity shops and Chinese takeaways that lined the main road running between my house and the park.

I didn't want a showdown but I had questions about the family silence, their awkwardness with me, that I hoped my big brother could answer. His doorless office was within walking distance but, to save myself from the downpour, I drove and called on my way to ask if I could stop by and see him.

Shmuel handled my father's business affairs and I knew he spoke to him regularly, making him the most 'in the know' about my parents' thoughts and something of a messenger. Speaking to Shmuel was easier than speaking to my father and I needed to talk.

I parked up on the road outside, brushed past the receptionist and staff he had installed downstairs, and headed up to his office. His desk sat in the bay window, with a swivel chair parked behind it, so that he worked with his back to the busy road, which I thought odd. Why wouldn't you want to look out of the window?

I was nervous. Shmuel has the natural inclination to be a tender man but he can also behave like a bully. There are four and a half years between us and he carries his own trauma and insecurities from our shared childhood. When he is challenged, he grows instantly, unpleasantly defensive. This defensiveness was only exacerbated by what he already knew about my own strengths and resourcefulness in situations like this. In fact, there were times when he had relied on them.

My mind flickered back to when Shmuel was nineteen and I was fourteen. It was April 2001, and we were living in Israel. Shmuel was waiting for a girl to be suggested for him to marry. My parents had spoken to a matchmaker. My father had then vetted the matchmaker's candidates and meetings had been arranged with the selected few. Shmuel was very keen for my parents to hurry up the process but my father, as my mother would say, was 'finishing his Murray Mints', which is to say that in his deliberately casual and sometimes maddening way, my father didn't share Shmuel's sense of urgency.

Eventually, Shmuel recruited me to try to find out what stage my father was at in his conversations. I tried to listen in on his phone calls but it wasn't easy; my father used to take them in the fortified room in our home, reinforced to protect us from rocket attacks. On one occasion, my father saw me trying to listen and promptly shut the door – it was impossible to hear through it. But I had seen him making notes in his notebook. That was my way in.

I knew exactly how to do it. He also wrote down holy Torah thoughts in that notebook, so he wouldn't take it into the bathroom with him, lest his holy Torah writings be in the presence of human nakedness. I waited for the first opportunity and then struck, feeling big and important as I read and remembered the names of the girls and the notes next to them, learning the list off by heart to repeat to my brother later.

Now, in his doorless office in Manchester, I wondered if my brother might be afraid of the ingenuity and resilience that he had previously relied on.

I wanted to ask him if anyone in the family still cared about me, because lately it felt like no one did. The bar mitzvah had left me wondering where I stood and, just the day before, I'd had a meeting with Zvi and not one of them had called to ask how it had gone. My head told me I was being frozen out but my heart wasn't ready to believe that. I had worked myself up on the drive over from Rachel's tirade, growing angrier and more upset as the seconds passed. By the time I arrived, my tone was confrontational. To Shmuel's mind, I was there for a showdown. For answers. But it was a dressing-down, not answers, that I warranted, as far as he was concerned. It was a matter of moments before our voices were raised.

Both of us knew how many people could hear us arguing, and this public sparring match made me feel even more alone than I already did. He had what felt like an army and allies around him, but maybe he felt alone too, a king with no equals, the chief executive of his self-made success.

He took pains to tell me that he was acting with my father's blessing and that he represented all of our six siblings when he spoke, even Miriam. Then, he leaned forward and looked right at me.

'You need to be told. You are a pig,' he said.

I laughed in his face – bitter, short, sharp. Bravado's laughter. To Jews, pigs are, of course, the most profane of all animals. Their flesh is forbidden because a pig lies on its back, in the mud, waving its little split hooves in the air. By doing this, it is *pretending* to be kosher, drawing attention to its cloven hooves, like those of animals that also chew the cud and that the Torah deems acceptable to eat. A pig is a devious trickster, it makes a mockery of the law, and that's why the law forbids us to eat bacon, ham or pork. At least that's what we are told.

My brother was shouting louder now. 'You say what you want and you do what you want. You are an embarrassment. You are crazy, you are cuckoo.'

I goaded him. 'What is it I'm doing that is so crazy?' I asked.

I was beginning to sense where this was going; what was unsaid. If I was going to have to answer to him, I wanted him to feel uncomfortable too. I had waited this long – it was going to be on my terms. He was going to face up to this accusation, not me.

'Say it,' I demanded. 'Say it,' I said again.

He faltered. He cocked his head, its receding hairline and closely clipped beard now tipped to the right. 'This thing. That you've decided you're a lesbian.'

He stammered over the word – *lesbian* – but he said it. I relaxed. However hard this was for me, there was a victory in hearing him acknowledge a reality that I knew now had been hidden within our family for too long. Hidden inside me. In my mind, I recalled, as I had many times, the bare acknowledgement of lesbians in Jewish law: 'mere licentiousness'. If there was one thing my brother was good at, it was outsourcing his morality to Jewish law.

'I never decided to be a lesbian, Shmuel,' I told him. Because who could or would choose this rejection for themselves?

The pair of us continued to bat my apparent transgressions and his latent bigotry back and forth like a table tennis rally. 'I used to feel sorry for you,' he said. 'I thought you were that way because you were abused as a child.'

The abuse. He just threw it out there, without care. He thought he was being gallant, offering the cruelty I'd been dealt as an excuse for my sins. The familiar numbness that still grips me every time I think about it dropped like a fire curtain, falling abruptly over my face, suffocating and blinding me all at once.

I was frozen, but he ploughed on. 'But now people are

telling me that you've said it's nothing to do with that,' he continued. A more inquisitive brother might have posed it as a question but, no, this was a statement.

'Do you know how hard this is for me?' he challenged. 'People see the two of you walking around the park, holding hands, and I have to find something to say to them. These people don't pay to live in this area to be exposed to that.'

So he did know. Of course he knew. How long had he known? What business was it of these people who saw us? I wondered.

'Oh, grow a pair of balls,' I spat out. 'Why do you need to answer to them?'

He had indeed grown afraid of my voice, my freedom. My strength.

His insults carried on, swirling in the air, jumping and swooping so fast that he tripped over his own words.

'You are not our sister any more,' he said, and then stopped short. He tried to cycle back. 'I will be nice to you as a human,' he offered, 'but not as a sister.'

I lost respect for him in that moment. Or maybe it was just that he no longer intimidated me. His shape shifted in front of me, from my familiar big brother who I thought could do anything, into a small, weak man. I wondered if he'd ever had any respect for me, at any point? I think he had pitied me, this sister who couldn't maintain a marriage and didn't fit into the shape of a woman as he knew it.

'Is this how you are nice to other humans?' I was shouting again.

'G-d wants me to speak to you this way,' he said, leaning back in his chair, slowing down as the words fell out of his mouth.

I wished I knew with such confidence exactly what G-d wanted of me at any given moment.

'You are not Charedi,' he threw at me, now inflicting pain.

I laughed through the snot and shock and tears that now streamed across my face. Who is Charedi, anyway? Charedi means 'he who trembles' (before G-d). It is meant to denote those who are in alliance with the most conservative end of orthodox Judaism. But it is an artificial term made popular as a way of waving our identity in people's faces so that our leaders can organize politically and financially. It is no one in our community and it is everyone in our community. Who was my brother to decide which? I didn't need anyone's permission to identify with the community that birthed me, educated me, married me, hurt me. I didn't need to agree with every value that is popularly held in order to use it as a shorthand for my birthright, my heritage. I cannot unsubscribe from the taste of my soul, from what is innately within me, no matter how many rules I break.

I could not breathe. I could not see. I could not think. Somehow I walked downstairs and stumbled out of the building and towards my car outside. It had been raining and the ground was slippery with wet, pink blossom that was turning brown. I unlocked the Yaris, opened the door and sat behind the steering wheel, but I knew I could not drive. I got out again and walked, blindly, along the pavement, past the Chinese takeaways, until I found myself in the park down the road, where I often took my children to play. My feet found their way to a heavily wooded area where the wet, woody scent of pine trees carried through the air. They found the space for me to cry. The summer rain was still coming down and I swatted away swarms of tiny midges from my face.

I walked around in circles in the mud and leaves. I was humiliated and afraid, and the little girl inside me thought that if I phoned my father, he would sort it out. He had never done so in the past, but it didn't stop me from hoping he would now. It never stopped me from hoping.

I pulled up his number in my phone, hovered over it, and hit the green call button. He answered from a cab on the way to the airport, heading back to Israel. I'd seen him only briefly on a passing visit to my house, where we muddled through a disengaged conversation. A couple of days after my niece's wedding, I'd seen him again when he took the kids and me for a meal in a kosher burger restaurant where, again, the well of conversation ran eerily dry. Suddenly I remembered the discussion with my mother about her bracelet and the urgency with which she handed it over. With clarity, I realized she knew that soon I would no longer be worthy, to them, of my inheritance.

Now, on the phone to my father, in the park, I could hear my mother in the background, directing their taxi driver to the airport. My father was halting, faltering, at first, because who wants to talk to their daughter about her sexuality, which, by now, we both knew was the purpose of my call and the reason for their distant behaviour. Nonetheless, he soon grew comfortable with berating me. He spoke in the voice he uses to talk to my aunt, whose life he doesn't approve of either, and settled into his familiar role as patriarch and dominant. He wielded religion and scripture, beating me with it like a stick. I knew religion and scripture too, but his voice was louder than mine. He was only on the phone; nothing or no one was making me continue to listen to him, but I did anyway. I still hoped he would help me, even though he was the one who had decided that my sexuality was a problem to begin with. Somewhere inside me, little Yehudis with her red leather shoes hoped he would save me. I knew what he would think but I desperately needed his kindness in that moment, for him to see me as his daughter. I was crying into the wind.

He asked me outright: 'Are you breaking the code of Jewish law?' And, then: 'Are you in a physical relationship with a woman?'

His words stunned me. I didn't expect him to be explicit. I thought he would use euphemisms: 'forbidden relationship', 'unnatural' or some other archaic expression. That's what he'd done when I had tried to tell him how hard married life had been for me, how I could not tolerate sex with Zvi, how it hurt, physically and emotionally – he'd used words palatable to himself to navigate the discomfort. It was jarring to hear him now, after all this time, ask me such a deeply personal question.

I tried to sidestep it. 'Have you ever asked Shmuel if he has broken the purity laws and hugged his wife while she was menstruating?' I asked out of no particular interest except to make a point.

He ignored me and repeated his question. 'Are you in a physical relationship with a woman?'

I was stuck. I didn't want to deny or dishonour my relationship with Hannah but neither did I want to engage with his trespass and dignify it with a response. It was the first time he had acknowledged her existence.

I felt small. I felt sick. I gave in. 'Yes,' I said.

He went quiet for a fraction of a second, missing just a beat, no more, then said: 'What did you expect me to say? You know the law. Maybe you'd hoped for something different from me, but you must have known that was just hope.' He knew he was being cruel.

'Repent', he instructed me, like the prophet Jeremiah. I stood silent. 'Your *shabbos* isn't worth keeping.'

This was a huge insult to me. I loved *shabbos* – he knew I did: the exhale, the peacefulness that settled into my home when the sky darkened on a Friday night until three stars appeared the following evening. I loved the new life it breathed into me as the day of rest faded and a new week began. My *shabbos* was part of what kept me in this community, why I refused to leave.

My *shabbos* wasn't his to take.

He threatened me. He said he would publicly announce that he disagreed with my choice. *To whom?* I wondered. Who would he tell? How did he think they would look at him, afterwards? We'd been on the phone for forty minutes, my mother intercepting with directions when needed but never part of the conversation. He arrived at the airport and one of us put down the phone. I don't remember who. No one said goodbye. I was still in the park, walking in circles in the mud.

My father, like Shmuel, had claimed G-d. They both thought that they had G-d on their side. But wasn't G-d big enough for all of us? I was certain that He was. I realized that my father was embarrassed of me. This man of G-d was too vain, too worried about what the neighbours would think, to love his own daughter for who she was. What else would lead him to be so ridiculous, to be so delusional in his own grandeur that he could stake a claim over G-d? This was shame; shame that he hid behind his faith. In the confines of our community, there is shame in failing to produce obedient, straight daughters. But G-d was big enough to obscure my deficiencies, alongside his.

Encircling the sodden leaves with the tracks of my shoes, I wondered where my mother had been during that call – mentally, emotionally. I'm certain that she never imagined the extent to which I'd choose not to conform or that the seeds of rebellion sewn in childhood would establish such roots. My questioning voice had grown far, far too loud in womanhood. My mother had always absented herself as soon as anything got difficult or complicated. I have a returning image, in my mind, of her standing over the kitchen sink in our childhood home, weeping into its suds as she washed the dishes. Not one of us ever asked why she was crying. We pretended it wasn't happening. I wonder now if that's what she had wanted us to do, or if it was just easier for everyone involved at the time? It's what she was doing in the taxi. Pretending it wasn't happening. It's what she'd taught all of us to do.

Still in the park, my phone rang. Hannah. She was in London and hadn't heard from me for hours. I had lost all track of time. I was also lost in the pine trees and the mud. I muttered, through tears, something about not being able to breathe and not knowing what to do next. She told me to go round to our friend Shevy's. Shevy lived locally and was always supportive.

On Hannah's instruction, Shevy called my phone and guided me out of the park. My feet found their way back to my car, still parked up outside Shmuel's office, and I drove the short distance to her home, where I sank down on her sofa with a mug of hot tea.

My lost-girl mentality ebbed away and was replaced with a renewed need for answers – but to different, new questions. I needed to understand what had just happened. I texted each of my older siblings to see if Shmuel was right, if he really had spoken on behalf of all of them when he told me that I wasn't their sister any more. I typed the words on the keypad of my phone: 'According to Shmuel, I am no longer part of this family, and all siblings are on the same page. Have you signed up to this?'

Each replied in turn. They told me that they loved me – but each now loved me with their own stipulations. They loved me but I embarrassed them. They loved me but I had exposed their children to sinful life choices, and this was a terrible, terrible thing. They loved me but I had changed and they wanted me to change back. This was not love as I understood it to be. As the replies rolled in, Shevy read them with me, holding me as I howled. I was so grateful for her strength.

Only Elchanan, the most religious and now a teacher, displayed a shred of humanity in his reply. As children, with three years between us, Elchanan used to adjust my nappy for me when I was far too old to be wearing one; well out of toddlerhood, our parents had forgotten to move me on from them. Elchanan was the only one I'd formally told about Hannah. When I'd arrived home from my most recent stay with him and his wife, in London, just a few weeks earlier, I had written an email to the two of them, telling them, in confidence, that I respected the pair of them too much to hide my relationship from them any longer. Hannah wasn't welcome in their home, they'd replied, but I still would be. This condition had upset me but I knew he'd had time to process – and he knew that I already knew his boundaries. Over text, he offered no more acceptance than he had over email, but he didn't mock me, either. He didn't dismiss me or tell me to change, as each of the others now did. It wasn't much, but at this point the bar for what counted as acceptance was low.

I read each message back as it came through. There had clearly been a siblings' meeting – minus me – that had preempted all the awkward, disengaged chat, the bar mitzvah and my conversation with Shmuel. I was still their sister, but their love no longer came with respect, acceptance, support, joy or kindness. When I think back now, I'm not sure that it ever did. All the things I now know to be the foundations of relationships worth having and holding on to were absent from my relationship with my siblings. Realizing this, I felt like I had lost all of my family in one fell swoop.

The reckoning was instant, and I was grief-stricken; it was as though they'd disappeared from the face of the earth. In that moment I learned, through the crude medium of WhatsApp, that their love was conditional. What a fool I was, and how small I felt to realize it. You can't love someone 'if', you can only love someone 'and'. Otherwise, it isn't love. Each member of my family was telling me they loved me *if* I conformed, *if* I obeyed. They loved me if I was quiet, if I lay back and thought of England, and if I performed heteronormativity inside the constructs that had raised us. Constructs that had failed me dismally, almost irreparably.

I resolved to myself that, in this family, from this day forward, my absence would have to count for my presence. Being where I would never be enough was too painful, and so I was releasing myself. I was accepting their awfulness and the fact that it wasn't mine to change. Just as I was not theirs to change – no matter how much they tried and no matter how hard they insisted. From hereon in, the space that I left would say more than I was ever allowed to.

There was one person that my family forgot to talk to about my abominations – my little sister Devorah. Growing up, we had been a pair, the two littlest girls, three years apart.

The morning after the reckoning, I had a phone call from her. I thought she'd been told but it quickly became clear she hadn't and was, in fact, just calling to check in, having been thinking of me. She knew nothing of what had gone on and, like me, had been left out of the family summit I felt sure had taken place.

'I was waiting for a call from you,' I started, still thinking she'd been informed.

Her response told me that she didn't know what I was talking about, and so I briefed her – about my relationship, about Shmuel's edict, about the texts.

'No one tells me anything,' she complained. Not a word more.

That day – that meeting, those messages, their responses – marked the end of something: my hope for acceptance. I had wondered and feared for so long how my parents would react to all of me. Now I knew. Contorting myself into religious heteronormativity had stifled me and sickened me for as long as I could remember, so much so that it was what had become safe and known to me. I deserved better than that but I hadn't realized it fully until then. In my decision to come out to my family, I'd only ever been thinking about and driven by what I thought Hannah deserved, how she was entitled to be acknowledged and respected as my life partner. That's what I thought I was fighting for and what had motivated me to stand up to my family's judgement. Lying about our relationship felt like I was disrespecting Hannah, even by omission, and it was not something I was willing to do any more. Through it all, I had never seen it as something I was doing entirely for myself. How wrong I was. Abandoning that hope, which even my father knew I was clinging on to, had breathed life into me. Coming out and facing the rejection that, deep down, I'd long known to expect from my family, had now breathed oxygen into mine and Hannah's relationship.

But every so often, from then until now, I bend over double, winded by the excruciating cost of my freedom.

19

Jolly good fellow, Part 2

יְהִי רָצוֹן שֶׁתְּהֵא מוֹרָא שָׁמַיִם עֲלֵיכֶם כְּמוֹרָא בָּשָׂר וָדָם

May (your) fear of Heaven be like your fear of flesh and blood.

Brochos, 28b

WITH EVERYTHING OUT IN THE open, loveless emails from my parents began dropping into my inbox. It started on a practical level: a large bill that landed and that I'd struggle to cover on my own. My father had been contributing towards it but I no longer knew where I stood, so I forwarded it to him to try to find out. If I was going to be covering the bill myself, I needed to work out how to afford it. I held on to the small hope that, despite his disapproval, he would stand by me, at least when it came to looking out for the children and their needs.

His response came three or four days later in an email asking me to read an attached letter from him, which he'd had approved by another rabbi. In it he described my life as an abomination and severe transgression. 'Loneliness is no justification,' my father wrote in a voice that sounded very much like my mother's admonishments.

The letter proceeded to hint at an 'idea' that they believed would help 'normalize' my situation. However, as long as I was in a relationship with 'that woman', it couldn't work, he wrote. I had no clue what this 'idea' was yet so I would have to wait to find out, but the message around it was clear as day: my relationship had become a talking point among everyone they knew and many they did not, and that was no good for them. My own reputation would be tarnished, he said, but they were adamant that they would not allow the esteem in which our family, beyond me, was held to be impacted by my decision not to live by the standards of the Torah.

'I have no choice but to tell all the family members not to talk to you about any private matter,' my father – actually my mother and father – wrote. It was, I had to accept, natural that they and my siblings should all be wary of my non-Torah ideas and wish to protect themselves and their families.

It was signed, 'Love, Daddy xxx' and each kiss felt like a further stab to my heart. He always did that, packaged up his admonishment in platitudes that only added to their cruelty.

The fullness, the depth of their rejection didn't sink in at first. Only as I read and reread the email over the following hours and days did the hurt seep into my soul. Each time, it was way shittier than I'd thought.

I cried over and over to Hannah on the phone and she advised me not to respond to the emails. I felt utterly abandoned by my parents. I was heartbroken.

I replied, telling them that I wouldn't engage with the hurtful things they were saying, and suggested we talk through a mediator. I awkwardly asked friends and acquaintances for a recommendation of someone who might be able to help me reach some kind of way forward with my parents and settled on one who seemed experienced both in her field and in the workings of our community. She and I spoke together first, but she'd had just one conversation with my father when she wrote back to me: 'It would not be ethical to pursue mediation in this case.' She said the content of the messages from my father were such that she wasn't willing to pass them on to me. I consulted a second mediator, who my mother agreed to see. The verdict, sent to me by this third party, was the same: 'In my professional opinion it would not be a good idea to engage with them.'

My father continued berating me in emails, explaining how I was the common denominator in my own misfortune, blaming me for all that happened in my life before I had even turned twenty years old.

'You'll be surprised how a little humility elevates one soul,' he wrote in one email, returning me to a condescension, a pain, that was so familiar from childhood. Through it all, he continued to hint that he had this 'idea' to fix things but that he knew I wouldn't listen. I still didn't know what 'it' was.

'There are no ideas that are going to make me not gay,' I replied.

If one thing grew from my family's rejection, it was my and Hannah's relationship. Faced with the reality that I no longer had my family to support me, I leaned into every nook and cranny of our life together. The need for this to be a viable alternative became pressing because I didn't think my psyche could withstand the loneliness if it wasn't. Hannah really showed up for me.

When my parents emailed or when Leah sent WhatsApp messages saying she didn't understand why I'd made the decision to be with Hannah, we'd go over every word together to help me try to make sense of sentences that felt senseless. When small things like heavy traffic or hurrying the children to appointments or looming university deadlines made me cry, Hannah would hold me or be on the other end of the phone just to be alongside me. She possessed a stillness I didn't know within myself. She was grounded, while I felt like I was in constant flight.

At the end of August, it was my birthday. Hannah sent me upstairs for a nap while she busied around the house with the children.

'We're conducting a science experiment, too messy for birthday girls to have to deal with,' she said as she ushered me up for the kind of comforting afternoon snooze that lets you wake up still enveloped in a warm daze. It was early evening when I walked back into our kitchen to find Grandma's avocado kitchen tiles studded with rainbow-flag decorations that the children had put up to celebrate me. There were cards from each child – handwritten wishes that reflected their personalities: funny and quirky from Roni, over-the-top from Talia, earnest and grateful from Noam. Presents, too, had been set on the table where we ate, specially picked out on a visit to TK Maxx with Hannah: a cream-and-orange throw, bath bubbles and a merino-wool jumper in deep green – items Hannah knew I would love, bought on our non-existent budget. I remembered how I felt when Miriam surprised me with the chocolate 'eight'. I loved Hannah for this, for all the thought and attention that had gone into finding my gifts.

There was a shiny, multicoloured helium balloon bopping against the ceiling and, for a moment, I saw it as myself, constantly trying to climb higher. It was tethered to a small weighted star and I thought about how Hannah grounded me.

They'd all baked and decorated a cake for me: two-tiered and smothered in what looked like twenty different types of chocolate, piled with fudge frosting and brown and white malted honeycomb balls, all under a shower of brightly coloured sprinkles. It was set on a heavy blue ceramic dinner plate, from the set I bought when I left Zvi. Hannah put it down in the middle of the table, with its one wobbly leg that needed a folded-up tissue wedged underneath to keep it from toppling. I could see the expectation in her face as it searched mine. Did she know how much this meant to me?

Finally, I thought. I was a jolly good fellow and I didn't need anyone else to say it.

A rabbi I'd known since childhood video-called to join in the celebration, smiling through my phone screen with his wife, Zissy. Rabbi Spielman was hardcore Chasidic and they had both known me since I was a baby. But he and his wife were also part of the new community we had begun building around us, people who shared our faith and also accepted us for *us*; people who admired me for my work and for staying. Rabbi Spielman wore a frock coat similar to my father's but with tiny differences in how the buttons were arranged and the way the darts were sewn that denoted their separate religious alliances. Zissy wore a headscarf and trendy glasses and we could see half of each of their faces as they crowded into the screen's view together. I blessed them both because I knew that on my birthday, I had the power to bestow blessings on others.

In the Jewish calendar it was Elul, the month leading up to Rosh Hashanah, the Jewish new year, one of the holiest and most joyful days in our calendar. It was a time of celebration that usually coincided with the end of the Gregorian August and the beginning of September, when the air turned crisp and everyone's step quickened. In Elul, we are commanded to listen to the unmistakable trumpeting sound of the *shofar*, a ram's horn with ceremonial use dating back millennia, blown every day at this time of year. It is a cry to awaken us in time for Yom Kippur, the Day of Judgement, eight days after the new year; to remind us to reflect and move on, as better people. Rabbi Spielman put one to his lips. It was short and curved, mottled brown and cream and polished to a high shine. Those who have learned how to do it can breathe sonic life into this otherwise inanimate object, with a sound so bracing it makes us stop and consider. It is a sound of both celebration and remembrance. He blew it and, in my kitchen, we were all, temporarily, silent. It lasted just a minute and a half, its sound greater and more commanding than when we had tried to blow it ourselves. I squeezed Hannah's hand under the table as we listened, to draw myself away from the past and into the present. Into the future.

A couple of months later, Hannah and I lay in bed, in Grandma's house, in Manchester. It was late, about 11.30 p.m., the kids were all asleep and we had the covers pulled up to our ears to keep out the cold. For the past year, since we had started picturing our future together, we had discussed getting engaged. My decision to confront my family had, in part, been in preparation for it – for moving in together and finally having Hannah by my side at family functions.

That night, we lay together and spoke about how we could make it happen. We talked pragmatically, pulling up our calendars on our phones and working out when, between my studies and her work and the kids' various needs, would be the right time to take this next step. We looked up from the dates on our screens and straight at each other, our faces lit up by the devices in our hand, like glow-worms in a dark room. What were we waiting for? we asked ourselves. The only people we needed to make that decision were right there, in bed together. We could get engaged now, in bed in our pyjamas, if we wanted.

'Don't you want a proposal?' Hannah asked, sitting up.

'Go on then,' I said, feeling like the luckiest person in the world. She held my face in both her hands and I held my breath.

'Yehudis Gittel Fletcher, will you marry me?' Hannah asked.

'Yes, Hannah,' I replied. 'Will you marry me?' She nodded.

We grinned at each other. I don't know who said it first but our next thought was the same: *Let's tell the kids.*

We knocked on their doors and woke them one by one, my three and Hannah's youngest, and the house filled with excited chatter about a family and a home and a wedding. Not just that, it filled with hope, too.

In the days that followed, we posted on our social media

pages that we'd got engaged and watched our inboxes fill with messages from people who loved us as a couple. Roni was excited about being called up in his school assembly, which was usual when a child had a family celebration but, pre-empting the school's reaction, I sent a text message to a teacher there who I considered a friend to let her know the situation – that Roni was full of beans because he knew that when there was a family *simcha* (joy), you got invited to the front so your schoolmates could wish you *mazel tov*.

She didn't reply but the headteacher did, later that day, with an email explaining that while the school did wish us *mazel tov*, they didn't want to compromise any of their 'priorities', so he wouldn't be calling them up or announcing their news in assembly. Instead, he would invite my children to his office and give them a celebratory sticker to wear on their uniforms. So, that's what they got: a private lecture on how their mother's love life was not in accordance with Torah values, sweetened with a sticker to pop on their navy-blue school sweaters nonetheless. The teacher–friend never spoke to me again, although her husband made a point of being polite when he saw me.

We had an engagement party in our local pub in Hendon a week later – the same one Hannah and I went to before *shul* on Friday nights. I wore a new pair of silver brogues that made me feel something special. We reserved the outside area and were joined by forty of our friends. The terrace was illuminated with outdoor lighting and heaters, and there were wooden benches and tables. As more people turned up, we pulled up extra bar stools to make room. Friends from all the different parts of our lives came together, many of whom had never met each other but had us in common. No one there had done this before – embarked on a lesbian marriage as Charedi women – so the atmosphere felt talismanic and triumphant. As the pub emptied out, a friend snapped a picture of Hannah and me from behind, standing on the tarmac, saying goodbye to one of our last guests. Hannah has her thumb hooked in the back pocket of my jeans and I have my arm around her shoulders. Charging between us is a sense of joy that we have made it this far.

We arranged a weekend away in Brighton – known as the queer capital of the UK – to celebrate. The budget wasn't much so we booked a Travelodge-type place near the centre, where we could spend a couple of days and nights together, without kids, just soaking up this very special time. We revelled in the feeling that we were on the cusp of creating a new family and a joint life for ourselves against all imaginable odds.

We arrived at the hotel the following Thursday night and, on Friday morning, our first morning there, I woke up to a phone call from Zvi. He had the kids so I picked it up instantly, afraid that something had happened to them. He knew about the engagement and had already congratulated us, so the words that came out of his mouth next – and their timing – surprised me.

'Your father's asked me to get back together with you,' he said.

What the fuck?

'Yeah,' he continued. 'He said he'll make it worth it for me.'

Again, what the fuck?

I could only presume my father – who, of course, I had

heard nothing from regarding my engagement – had offered him money, or some other incentive, as Zvi relayed how he'd emailed him and then set up a Zoom call to discuss an idea that might help the family. So *this* was the idea that my parents had been hinting at in their emails to me. I felt filthy. My father knew what had happened in my marriage; he had sat there and helped me to get out of it. Now that he didn't like the version of Yehudis that emerged, he'd decided that a *frum*, miserable family was a better look for the children than a mother liberated from her husband. How could he entertain the idea that this would somehow be good for me?

I messaged my mother: 'I'm literally campaigning against forced marriage and this is what you're doing.'

Hannah and I returned to our weekend but the back-and-forth of angry messaging with my parents resurfaced when we got home.

With Hannah back in London and me in Manchester, we took up daily love-lettering.

'To my beautiful human,' Hannah would write, or 'To my beautiful fiancée', as we exchanged emails about missing each other and how we couldn't wait to live together and grow old together. 'I wonder whose hair will go grey first,' she wrote on days when I needed to laugh, or 'I see your pain' at the times when I cried to her about my family.

In November, we attended my first lesbian wedding, between two of Hannah's friends, one a rabbi in a liberal community and the other a cantor who led the prayers in the synagogue. Both wore big white wedding dresses and it took place in a marquee in the grounds of a country hotel near Nottingham. Hannah and I spent the day there among other gay couples and friends who celebrated them wholeheartedly without any hint of rejection or animosity. It was an explosion of what was possible.

It was around a month later, with Manchester gripped by December's reliable freeze, when I went downstairs to lock up one evening and noticed a handwritten envelope on the doormat with no stamp. I bent down to pick it up and recognized Shmuel's handwriting across the front, in blue biro. I took it upstairs to the kitchen and tore it open. I looked at the first paragraph and glanced to the name at the bottom . . . Daddy. He had clearly had Shmuel write the envelope to make sure I opened it. I cast my eyes back up to the top again to continue. He wrote about a passage from the second book of the Prophets, Judges: Chapter 11, which tells the story of Yiftach, a father so committed to G-d that he promised his only daughter as a sacrifice. Yiftach was a fighter so eager for G-d's guarantee of success as he went into battle that he promised to offer up whoever or whatever first came out of his home on his return. When his daughter emerged, he followed through with his vow.

I'd heard that story a hundred times as a child and I'd studied the text as I grew older, but it was beyond my imagination for my father himself to put us into that story. I read it over and over again. What was he saying? Was he saying he was going to kill me? Like Yiftach? Sacrifice me for my sins? I tried to read it every which way but I couldn't ignore the terror coursing through me now as the words left the page. Even if his meaning was something different, it was, at the very least, intended to make me feel scared. What other conclusion could I draw from a story about a father killing his daughter?

I reached his sign-off: 'With love from your old Dad xxx'. It knocked me sideways.

I called a support worker I knew whose job was to help victims of honour-based abuse. She reported my letter to the police and an officer called the next day. I remember him asking me: 'What does Judges 11 say exactly?'

When I told him how Yiftach had cut a deal with G-d to murder his daughter he strongly urged moving me and the children to a shelter. I couldn't shake the idea that, to my father, maybe a dead daughter was better than a gay daughter but, at the same time, I simply couldn't imagine him taking that step. I chose to believe that he was more invested in frightening me than hurting me and that his goal was, ultimately, to bully me into listening to him. We chose to stay at home but every last vestige of respect that I'd ever held for him left me in that moment. The police asked that my brother not contact me again. But in January, he did.

20

Home

אֶבֶן מָאֲסוּ הַבּוֹנִים הָיְתָה לְרֹאשׁ פִּנָּה

The stone that the builders rejected has become the chief cornerstone.

Psalms 118:22

AN EMAIL DROPPED IN MY inbox from Shmuel via a generic office address belonging to his property company. The subject line was my address – the address of Grandma's mews – and I wondered if it was an appointment to check the gas certificate or something equally mundane.

'Dear Yehudis . . .' it started.

Shmuel had called me Gittel his whole life, so if this was a personal note from him, it wasn't our usual level of correspondence. I read on. The email explained that he and my parents were putting the house, my and the children's home, on the market. They planned to do so in the not too distant future and to sell it vacant on completion. They were writing to talk through a timetable that would have me out by spring.

'Please come back to us with a timescale you think you can work to,' it said, and asked me to get in touch with the estate agents they'd instructed to conduct the sale. Shmuel signed it on behalf of his property company as managing agents.

I was seated at the kitchen table, in front of my laptop, where I'd been working on a final-year essay. I had half a year left at university – six months left living on student finance – and they wanted to evict me? After everything that had already passed between us, they wanted to upend everything I'd worked for and take the roof from over my and my children's heads right now? I wondered if this was all coming from Shmuel and my father; I couldn't believe that my mother had signed off on it, not for her mother's house, not for her daughter's home. I sent her a text with a screenshot of Shmuel's email and wrote: 'Just in case you don't know about this, this is where things have got to.'

She replied quickly and curtly. This was what needed to be done, she said. She was sure I'd be OK. I wrote back equally quickly: 'Never contact me or my children again.'

I felt utterly betrayed. How had they sunk this low to punish not just me, but their own grandchildren? The panic over where we would live and how I would afford it was instant. I was trying so hard to complete my degree and succeed in my advocacy, where I'd just found my stride, and, now: eviction. I couldn't imagine how I'd do it. I pleaded with them for an extension, beyond spring, until my degree was complete that summer. They agreed to it, but a week later my father messaged from my mother's phone – somewhat heeding the police warning not to be in direct contact – to deliver another sucker punch. Until this point he had been plugging the rent gap to help me afford the place. Between now and the sale of the house, he would no longer supplement the expense, leaving me to find an additional £300 a month to pay my bills. 'I hope that you will regret what you have said and done,' he wrote.

For years, I had budgeted to the last penny for my family, so this was literally food out of my children's mouths. My own parents were doing this to us – rendering us homeless to make their point.

I suspected that, underlying it all, they didn't want to be seen as endorsing my sins by enabling me to live within the community. That would make them complicit. Awkwardly for them, British law looks unkindly at those evicting people on account of their sins, but I was tired. I had not stopped clawing for space in my community but I had learned where to expend my energy doing it. I didn't want to fight them any more. If they thought it made them powerful by inflicting hardship on me and my children, I found power in divesting myself of the last remnants of dependency on them. I agreed that I would move as soon as I had handed in my dissertation. In the meantime, I would have to find a way to pay the bills.

I couldn't take on any more days at work and I had to get my dissertation finished; both of those things, on top of the kids, were draining all of my time. I was desperate, though, *really* desperate. I seriously considered sex work and chat lines. A friend told me she'd done it, that she had one elderly client who she only had to see once every three months and all he wanted was to watch while she and another girl had sex. *Could I do that?* I asked myself. When I told my friends what was going through my mind, a couple of them formed a little committee and we met to strategize. They asked me to work out the financial gap that I was facing from the increased rent, from then until the time I had to move. It was another seven months, so over £2,000. Within days, one of them dropped a GoFundMe link in our WhatsApp chat – they had set up a fundraiser, titled 'Help stop a single mother from getting evicted for being gay'. By the time my friends, and then their friends, had forwarded it to a bunch of their groups, the little battery bar was quickly climbing towards its target. It was complete by the time the week was out, full of hundreds of small donations. Finally, I was not alone.

Though life threw new challenges at me, the old ones never went away. I was notified that Todros was due a parole hearing in a month's time. He had been in prison for seven years now and I was asked to submit a victim impact statement that would help to determine the conditions of his release.

I gave my evidence via a video call, with Hannah and two friends sitting on the couch beside me as I perched on an old chair at my dining room table. I'd sat at that table as a child, eating my grandma's chopped liver spread on to challah. Todros's smarmy solicitor was on the call even though I'd been promised he wouldn't be, and that felt like another familiar trespass. I described the impact his crimes had continued to have on me, emotionally, sexually, practically, financially, in the years since he committed them and since the trial; how difficult it had always been for me to sleep; how I'd worked with therapists to control my thoughts during the day but still they manifested themselves in nightmares; how difficult I'd found it to establish a healthy, sexual relationship.

When I closed the lid on the twenty-minute call, I dissolved into my friends.

In the days that followed, I felt as though my last defences had finally been dismantled. I had appealed Todros's release and made my case but I knew it was inevitable he would soon be walking the streets again. My kids were bigger now, so trying to delay it wasn't just about protecting them but the community I wanted them to grow up in. I became agitated and even less able to sleep than before. The pain of my family's rejection, compounded by the horror of my past and fears for the future, felt too much. Hannah nourished me with bowls of homemade soup while I quietly got through my work, daily tasks and parenting. For the school holidays, I took the kids to a Butlin's holiday park in the south of England and steadily brought myself back to life. I packed kosher freezer meals and instant noodles to eat; we swam, zip-lined, made slime and sat on a freezing-cold British beach. It all reminded me what I was capable of and what I had to continue fighting for.

The months were ticking by. When Passover arrived, in April, Hannah and I hosted Seder – the festival meal – in Manchester. It would be my last *yom tov* (Jewish holiday) in Grandma's house, in my home, but we had decided that once I was thrown out, we would find a home together. This meal marked another start for our family. We invited some friends, including the one set of neighbours who'd told me about the 'not Yehudis' WhatsApp group: Vera, who was in her nineties and still exceptionally glamorous, always made up with lipstick and a wig (worn for vanity rather than religious reasons), and her daughter, Mel, who was in her seventies and had an almost daily gym habit. They were Jewish but not *frum* like the rest of the mews' inhabitants. On sunny days, they would both strip down to bikinis and sit outside the front of their home while the kids and I gathered on the swinging bench that I'd installed outside our garage next door. Vera and Mel cared for us and the feeling was mutual.

On Wednesday 11 May, I learned in a letter from the probation service that Todros was being released on licence. I'd done my level best to keep this community safe; at some point I had to accept this wasn't my responsibility, that it was up to them now. He wasn't allowed in the area but I felt stressed, sure he wouldn't respect the exclusion zone. I wrote on Twitter: 'Today marks an ending and a beginning. I will never forgive those who enabled his abuse, either passively or actively, either with their actions or their silence.'

Followers, people in the community and charities and advocacy groups, all got in touch, even rabbis who had been antagonistic in public but shown private support for my work. 'Shocked by legal decision,' my mother wrote in a text message. I wasn't sure what to make of that. It didn't offer me comfort.

I poured the remainder of my energy into my dissertation. I didn't know it then but I was delivering a brilliant piece of work. It examined evidence of safeguarding risk factors in my community. I just wanted it to make a difference, to have real world implications for policy and practice in Charedi communities like my own.

In August, I got a WhatsApp message from my university supervisor who had been grading my dissertation, urging me to check the university intranet. I'd got a first. 'You can feel validated,' he wrote. I read and reread his message. My own achievement filled me with happiness. Three years earlier, I didn't know how to write an essay; now, I not only had a degree, I'd turned into a scholar. I'd produced knowledge that could be put to use and I felt proud. I felt seen, too, because, along with my degree, I left with the university's 'Rising Star' Women's Voice award. After a life of longing for knowledge, university had been everything I'd hoped for and much more.

In the background, Hannah and I had been searching for a place to live. The only upside of being thrown out was that it expedited our decision to move in together, and we began booking viewings through the local estate agents. Naturally, in an area where all the tenants were Charedi Jews, the landlords were, too. We'd turn up for viewings, they'd take one look at us and ask: 'Are you living together?'

'Yes,' we'd answer, then find that the house that was available when we knocked on the door a moment earlier now miraculously wasn't.

At one property, which was falling apart and had no working plumbing, the agent, on discovering we were moving in together, offered: 'Take it as it is or don't take it at all.'

No one wanted to be the agent who gave a house to the couple that neighbours didn't want living next door. But I didn't want to go somewhere new, to leave this area that was home. I had already lost so much that I couldn't bear to lose anything else. Neither of us wanted to be anywhere but a Jewish area and we didn't want to take our kids out of Jewish schools. Despite everything, we still wanted our faith to be a core tenet of our family life, and that was non-negotiable.

To geographically leave my area would have felt like relinquishing my place in the community, but I was becoming increasingly worried that we wouldn't find anywhere.

I was beginning to lose hope until, in mid July, a friend saw an advert for a house a few streets away. She knew the landlady and I called immediately. It turned out I already knew of her myself – her husband was from Glasgow and his father had been the handyman that my parents used to do odd jobs around our home. I didn't let on too much about who I was, however; she would have known my story and I didn't know what side of the fence she fell on, in terms of her opinion of me.

I arranged to see the house the following Monday morning.

In front of me stood a slightly crummy-looking semi-detached, with once-white paint peeling from the window frames and a crudely put together garage extension made of corrugated iron. There was a short, narrow driveway bordered by a mature garden and overgrown hedge. It wasn't beautiful but at this point I just needed a roof over my children's heads and I hoped the woman who owned this place might be kind enough to give us one.

I had been asked to ring the bell of the house next door. A woman named Amanda opened the door, all smiles with a warm, sing-song South African Jewish accent. She wore a snood and had twinkly blue eyes. She told me she was a registered foster carer and that her current tenants had been Jewish refugees from the war in Ukraine who were about to continue to America. They had been very temporary and she was looking for their replacement.

We walked next door together and she announced herself

as she turned the key in the lock. There were two bedrooms and the garage was converted into a third. As I made my way through the house, I saw children variously sleeping and playing. She told me there were ten of them altogether, some at home and some who'd been slotted into local schools. I thought, if their mother can fit this many children in, then our blended family of six will fit in just fine.

Amanda showed me the garden with its two apple trees and the kitchen, which, while tiny, caught the light from all sides, through generous windows. *This could be a home for us*, I thought. We walked back to Amanda's and I knew this was the time to be explicit; I didn't want to sign for this home and then have it taken away when Amanda and her husband found out who we were. We sat down in her garden to take in the fresh air.

'I want you to know that my partner's a woman,' I said.

'Ah,' she said. 'So you *really* need a place to live.'

She'd been inundated since posting the advert and was still taking calls from people as we spoke. She cancelled them all.

'You need it more than they do,' she said. 'I don't know if I would come to your wedding but one of my good friends is gay and I'm OK with it. We like all sorts of people.'

I had taken a video to show Hannah and sent it over as I sat there.

'I wish I could find something more modern,' I typed.

'It's what we have,' she replied. At £1,000 a month, it was within our budget. We went for it.

On 25 August, three days before my thirty-fifth birthday, we moved out of Grandma's house and into our new home. It was disorientating seeing the house empty of all my things, watching my world as I'd known it since leaving my marriage disintegrate in front of me. But we had a new world to assemble now.

The children loved the responsibility of arranging their bedrooms and Amanda arrived with a huge tinfoil dish containing roast chicken and potatoes. We made a makeshift table out of a still-full cardboard box and the six of us – plus the two removal men – sat around among boxes full of my books and pictures, and our hastily reassembled sideboard, for our first meal as a family in our new home. We tucked in to the food using disposable cutlery and plates that we balanced on our knees. Of course, Hannah and I had our first argument, over the location of the fridge. But I looked around at my kids and the boxes full of my life in a place I called home, right in the heart of my community, and I felt invincible. I was going to be OK.

EPILOGUE

Daring to Stay

ותאמר יהודית שמעוני אחי הנה יזמתי לעשות דבר אשר לא יסוף זכרו לדור ודור

Then Yehudis said to them, 'Listen to me and I will do something which will be remembered throughout all generations among the children of our nation.'

Judith 8:30

Shabbos WAS FORTY MINUTES AWAY and Hannah and I were expecting thirty around our dinner table.

It was March, a few months before we moved into our first home together, and we were hosting in Hannah's rented ex-council house in London.

The smell of roast chicken and soup bubbling on the stove drifted through the small kitchen, tangling with the scent of early spring rain that made its way through the window, open just a crack to let in the breeze.

Gathering people around our table had become a tradition

of ours, taking it in turns since we'd first got together, to bring together anyone who wanted company on Friday nights. As the numbers grew, a community emerged of other people like us: gay or trans Jewish women and men, young and old, all of whom either came from orthodox Jewish communities or were still part of them and were thirsty for a space where all the parts of themselves belonged. I took pride in that space that we carved out together and delivered, with all the joy and comfort that it brought.

In adulthood, as in childhood, the peaceful wash of *shabbos*, starting with the Friday-night meal, never stopped being the highlight of my week. It was what I built, parented and worked towards in the six days in between. As a little girl, they were my week's *siyut* (climax); when I was married, the guests I invited to join my family created a structure that helped me to get through; when I met Hannah, these meals began to represent my future, a place of no great glamour or esteem but where no one had to choose. At my *shabbos* table, our sexuality and our heritage complemented one another beautifully, easily, successfully.

We set to work putting clutter aside and pushing together enough small folding tables to form a single large one. We placed the largest in the centre, its top made of grey plastic, with feeble metal legs that folded inwards, and two more, borrowed from a friend, were set lengthways, with a small wooden table that was usually Hannah's work desk tacked on to the end. We only had folding chairs, red and grey metal ones, but we'd borrowed more and as there wasn't room for a breath between them, we leaned each of them, still closed, against the table so they could be opened just as people sat down. One person would have to sit on the end on a twirly office chair brought down from upstairs.

We spread three white tablecloths, slightly mismatched, over the length of our assembled table and laid out thirty sets of unmatched cutlery, tumblers and wine glasses, each touching the next. We placed rainbow-striped serviettes under the forks, then stepped back and paused. Light and calm descended over the room.

It was approaching 6 p.m. and *shabbos* was minutes away now. Hannah checked on the chickens cooking in the oven and I ran upstairs, jumped in the shower, then pulled on navy pinstriped slacks and a white Oxford shirt. Hannah had changed into grey chinos and a patterned dress shirt. We looked at each other and grinned. We made a hot couple.

Downstairs, we lit the *shabbos* candles. We didn't have the silver candlesticks that had been given to us each as newlyweds – our husbands had kept those – but we lit two tea lights, precariously arranged on a piece of tinfoil set on top of the microwave. I always kindled the flames, whether in Hannah's house or mine, lighting the match and watching warm yellow glows emerge from the two wicks, then lacing my fingers, covering my eyes with my interwoven hands and saying the first sabbath prayer, with Hannah by my side: 'Blessed are you, G-d, who commanded us to light the *shabbos* candles.' Hannah and I wished each other 'good *shabbos*' and kissed.

As if on cue, our guests began to arrive. Some rang the bell while others knocked, depending on how observant they were of *shabbos* rules. We didn't care if they were *frum* or if they weren't. As the last of them arrived, after the prayer service at *shul* had ended, the smell of cologne wafted in and blended with the mixture of scents that already lingered in the air inside the house.

A lot of them knew each other, some didn't, but they all knew why they were there and a camaraderie immediately wrapped itself around each person who walked through the door. The sounds of their voices grew as new faces arrived and worked out who knew who and from where while Hannah and I poured and passed around drinks – gin and tonics, glasses of vodka and orange, wine – to friends who filled the narrow hallway, milled around the kitchen where the food was cooking or found a spot on the stairs to sit and talk.

I looked around and saw each guest in our assembly as thrilled as the next to find a *shabbos* table where they could be themselves. They included our doctor friend, who had come out as gay when he was young and was as familiar a face at our *shabbos* table as we were at his, and the two young women, university students in their early twenties, who were both observant and excited by what Jewish life could be when they joined our meals. Friends who were charity workers were chatting with a primary school teacher; a student rabbi with great capacity for joking and getting drunk joined them and told them about his studies and how he would soon be ordained within Judaism's less restrictive Reform movement.

Then there was Ed, who was in his seventies and possessed the manners of a true gentleman. He had seen homosexuality legalized in the UK and brought wisdom to our table, as well as a little sadness on account of this being the first time he had found Jewish acceptance like this.

'Look at this community and freedom that you have,' he said to me.

We ushered our guests through to the dining room and encouraged them to unfold and sit down on their metal chairs. Hannah took a seat at one end and I took the chair to her left. We'd all move around more than once before the night was done.

Hannah stood to make *kiddush* and everyone followed, rising to their feet as they sanctified the wine, reciting the prayer that my father used to say aloud: 'Blessed are You, G-d, ruler of the universe, who creates the fruit of the vine.'

'Amen,' we returned, in chorus, and each drank from the glass of whatever we'd poured.

I announced that I was going to wash and whoever wanted to follow should do so. I had long since stopped ritually washing before meals, finally indulging entirely the curiosity I'd carried since I was six years old and stood over the sink of the Fisher Price kitchen in the classroom above the *shul* hall. This was except for *shabbos* meals, of course. On *shabbos*, that holy, tranquil window which I so loved, I *chose* to wash before I ate, and while it had never grown into my favourite thing to do, this was a ritual that, once a week, I kept, with a full heart – but this time with room-temperature water and a fluffy hand towel.

Half of the guests chose to follow me into the small, square kitchen. I filled a lipped cup that we kept by the sink with water and felt the cold rush pour over my palms and down my wrists. I washed my right hand, twice, then my left, twice again. I walked back to the dining room and into a silence held for those of us who had washed, and raised the two challah loaves together in the air. I breathed in and spoke aloud to make the blessing over them, then gave them to Hannah to slice. The guests began to pass around the slices. I took a bite: the dough was delicious, pillowy and sweet, bought from the kosher bakery across the road from Hannah's house that morning. The poppy seeds from its crust tumbled down my front.

We made our way through courses of food that Hannah and I had spent days pondering and assembling, googling recipes and spamming each other with WhatsApp links for dishes that could cater for thirty guests, all with different diets. We'd settled on a menu of mock chopped liver (to satisfy the vegetarians) and egg salad topped with golden fried onions, followed by smooth butternut squash soup, a nut roast and several roast chickens.

All thirty of us ate and chatted and shared stories, in small groups and across the whole table, as the hours flew by. It was 10 p.m. before we served up the main course, and as we got more and more tipsy, the chatter grew louder, the room warmer and the talking turned into singing at every opportunity. These were the best kind of *shabbos* meals.

We sang the same songs that my father used to sing: ancient poems set to music about the ways in which we observe and celebrate. Their tunes had been passed down through families for generations and now they were ours. The room pounded like one big organism. Hannah drummed a steady beat, with her hands, on the table, and others thumped along with joy. Some were call-and-response songs where the doctor and I took the lead – neither of us were shy. The whole thing had taken on a life of its own. A big, unselfconscious frenzy.

Among us that night was a rabbi who was visiting London

from America. He turned to me in between verses: 'I've never been at a table like this where the Jewish spirit and the gay spirit are both so alive,' he said.

The time passed without us noticing. Small groups broke off into their own conversations as people took seconds and thirds from the serving platters that filled the table. I looked around at what I'd assembled, at these friends who all knew what it was to belong and not to belong at the same time, and took a quiet, solitary moment in my mind as the gathering pulsated around me. I was no longer the only Jewish lesbian at a table, I no longer hid, I no longer folded myself into the versions that G-d or my family or anyone else required of me. I had changed the topography of a community by showing others that a Charedi world could include lesbians, that a child could graduate into adulthood knowing what it looked like to be different but to stay. Knowing that it was a possibility. I was an activist, now, an accidental one but an activist nonetheless, and I was making changes that would benefit people long after me.

We stayed at the table until 2 a.m. Bottles of wine were emptied, plates were scraped clean then piled up by the sink and ignored. The room around me represented ultimate belonging and, even as our friends filtered out, one by one, into the stillness and darkness of London's earliest hours, the feeling we had all forged remained.

Hannah and I closed the door on our last guest and collapsed against it together. We looked over at the mess that engulfed the table and spilled on to the floor, and decided, without saying a word, that we could leave it until morning. We went upstairs and fell into bed.

I knew peace.

Acknowledgements

My biggest thanks go to Deborah Linton, who has been by my side since this project began. She has been my scribe, confidant and, most of all, my friend. Without you, your talent for storytelling and your eye for detail, Deborah, there would be no book. Thank you, NG, for introducing us.

Thank you, also, to my agent Kate Evans, who believed in *Chutzpah* when it was only an idea. Your guidance has been invaluable and I would not be here without your encouragement.

Thank you to Sharika Teelwah at Transworld for seeing the power my story has and putting it into the world, platforming it with such grace and respect. Thank you to KC Onuorah and Eva Maria Chacole, also at Transworld, for editing, suggesting, querying, and hearing my story with such care, and to Victoria Simon-Shore, Alex Newby, Barbara Thompson, Oliver Martin and Eloise Austen. A special thanks to Marianne Issa El-Khoury and James Jones for creating such a stunning cover despite all sorts of roadblocks.

The support group at Migdal Emunah was a haven for me, right back in its early days when we met in a tiny room at Hendon Library. Having been under Yehudis Goldsobel's leadership for ten extraordinary years, Migdal Emunah gave me my life back.

Thank you to Jo, Anne and the team at Greater Manchester Police for investigating the crimes committed by Todros Grynhaus, and to Brian and Alistair for prosecuting him with dignity and decorum. Thank you to the judge and other members of the courtroom staff, and last but not least, to the jury, unpaid members of the public who had to sit and listen to what he had done. I will never forget what you all gave me: my voice.

Thank you to Sally and the team at Mavar, to J at Salford Women's Aid, to L'chaim Food Bank, and to Simon. All givers should give in the way you did.

Thank you to those who knew me as a child and have taken the opportunity to get back in touch. I've had nothing but love and support from you and it means the world to me.

Thank you to my dearest friends, without whom I doubt I would be where I am today: AS, BG, BK, FW, GS, GH, HW, RO, Prof. RF and SB. For the meals, shoulders to cry on, the wisest of advice. I couldn't be luckier. And thank you to the Twisted Sisters – CF, EH and RH. You have all known and loved so many different versions of me. I love you all.

My deep gratitude also goes to Alexandra, who has been by my side through so much of this story, quite literally picking up the pieces when I felt I just could not put one foot in front of the other.

Thank you to Benjamin and the whole *frum*/ex-*frum* LGBT Friday-night dinner *chevre*. You show me what community is meant to look like.

To my family of Nahamu trustees, current and former: Benjy, Benjamin, Daniel, David, Doreen, Leigh and Nicola – thank you for your vision, foresight, temerity and, most of all, your friendship. Rashad, I'm including you as an honorary trustee. Eve, you, Josh and the kids have opened your home and heart to me. Thank you for your warmth, sisterhood and never-ending pragmatism.

Judith and Jane, thank you for accepting me and supporting me, for being my role models and dear friends.

To the three rabbis in my life: J and R, thank you for keeping me faithful; E, thank you for even more than that.

Thank you to 'Hannah', for being my catalyst.

To my precious, glorious children, 'Noam', 'Talia' and 'Roni'. You are the air I breathe. Thank you for your patience, your gorgeousness and your well-timed quips. I could not be prouder of who you are.

Thank you, also, to the others, who challenged me, hurt me and, no doubt, who I hurt too. My pain has forged me.

To Mummy and Daddy, and all my siblings: thank you for trying, even if it wasn't enough.

'No one should have to choose between staying and staying safe.'

Who is Nahamu?

Nahamu was founded by Yehudis Fletcher and Eve Sacks. It is supported by a board of trustees who have expertise in Jewish life, civic processes and community cohesion. All are deeply involved in the Jewish community and are committed to Jewish life and values.

Why was Nahamu founded?

British Charedi communities are sources of incredible strength and value to those who live in them. It is vital that they continue to flourish.

Nahamu's concern is that many who live in Charedi communities are increasingly subject to the unacceptable restriction of their autonomy and the violation of their rights as citizens of the United Kingdom. Many also feel that their best interests are not always advanced by an unaccountable hierarchical leadership. In pursuit of what those leaders sincerely believe to be the interests of those communities, communal leadership may promote conduct that causes harm: by denying educational opportunities, fostering ignorance, covering up abuse, normalizing forced marriage and creating a culture in which criminal conduct is necessary in order to survive.

Charedi communities around the world are struggling with these challenges. It is essential that we confront the systemic hurdles to the success of the Charedi community. We need solutions that address the harms which community members suffer, and to assist in the transition of the community to a model that will enable all members, and the community as a whole, to build a viable future. It is not sufficient to provide 'escape routes' for the minority of individuals who are determined to leave and are capable of doing so. Instead, we must provide systemic solutions for those who are trapped in an unsustainable way of life, or those who are denied freedom, education and choice.

Nobody should have to choose between staying in their community and staying safe.

What does Nahamu do?

Nahamu has raised concerns relating to these issues with religious and lay leaders across the community and has amplified the stories of those trapped within lifestyles that do not meet their needs. We have discovered a widespread lack of awareness of and a reluctance to engage with these challenges. We founded Nahamu in order to act as a focal point for advocacy within the Jewish community and to engage with policy makers and public bodies, so that together we can find an effective solution to the failings within Charedi communities.

Nahamu fights for the right of every Jewish person to live a life that is guided by their religion, without sacrificing their personal autonomy or welfare. We support those who wish to live a full and sustaining life of religious observance in the community that they have chosen, as well as those who wish to make changes to their lifestyle or move to a different part of the community. It is the right of every British citizen to practise their religion and experience their culture as they see fit. In turn, they should not cause harm to others through the practice of their religion. We wish to ensure that members of all religious communities have access to education that is key to ensuring a sustainable and viable future without conflicting with the law of the land. We believe that autonomous choice is critical to achieving that change. We believe that everyone should be able to exercise this choice without intimidation, coercion or undue influence. We believe that there are models and precedents that have been developed both in the UK and abroad that can provide us with guidance and optimism for the future.

You can find out more at www.nahamu.org.
Our registered charity number is 1195623.